WEALTHYAIRE

How to Build Economic Endurance

www.wealthyaire.com

Limits of Liability, Disclaimer of Warranty and Medical Disclaimer

The author and publisher shall not be liable for your misuse of the enclosed material. This book is strictly for informational and educational purposes only. The purpose of this book is to educate and entertain. The author and/or publisher do not guarantee that anyone following these techniques, patterns, suggestions, tips, ideas, or strategies will become successful or wealthy. The author and/or publisher shall have neither liability nor responsibility to anyone with respect to any loss or damage caused, or alleged to be caused, directly or indirectly by the information contained in this book.

Furthermore, the medical or health information in this book is provided as an information resource only you and is not to be used or relied on for any diagnostic or treatment purposes. This information is not intended to be patient education, does not create any patient-physician relationship, and should not be used as a substitute for professional diagnosis and treatment.

Usage of Bible References

References marked 'NASB' are from the New American Standard Bible® (NASB), Copyright © 1960, 1962, 1963, 1968, 1971, 1972, 1973, 1975, 1977, 1995, by The Lockman Foundation. Used by permission (www.Lockman.org)

References marked 'Amplified Bible' are from the Amplified® Bible (AMP), Copyright © 2015, by The Lockman Foundation Used by permission (www.Lockman.org)

References marked 'TPT' are from The Passion Translation® New Testament with Psalms, Proverbs, and Song of Songs, are used on a fair use basis by kind permission of the Broadstreet Publishing Group, LLC.

DEDICATION

This book is dedicated to God the Father, the Ancient of Days who sits upon the throne; Jesus Christ, our Chief Apostle and Prophet; and the Holy Spirit of God who is my mentor and ministry partner, the source of all true revelation, and the one who reveals himself as the seven Spirits of God (Isaiah 11:2).

ACKNOWLEDGEMENTS

My inspiration for writing this book has come from multiple sources:

Firstly, God has always been the beginning and end of my inspiration and secondly, my parents Mr Samuel Sunday Ugwu and Ms Ngozika Caroline Ugwu have been a major factor in ensuring that I remained inspired throughout the process of writing this book.

Several entrepreneurs whose brilliant work I have devoured and spent thousands of hours poring over - many of whom I have mentioned in this book and in my references. All of whom have been sources of great inspiration to me.

The wise Bible, business and science teachers I have sat under, and still sit under, together with the wonderful team at the Aaron group - efficiency and excellence describe their high-standard approach to completing a project.

My special family, Uchenna Samuel and Shalom Samuel, whose support and love have always been a scaffold to me, and who cannot be left out of the list of those who inspired me on this project.

So many beautiful people have significantly affected the quality of this book. These include Raymond Aaron, Dr Lance Wallnau, Ray Edwards, Dr Clement N. Ugwu, Sean Edwards, Steve Scott, Matthew Kimberly, Deri Llewellyn-Davies, Dillion Dhanecha, Rob Moore, Vishal Morjaria, Mark Davies, David Rogers, Loral Langemeier, Tony Cox, Tom Falconer, Kevin Hicks, Mark Waller, Matt Dearsley and David A. Reynolds

Finally, I can't forget my friends: there are many of them who encouraged me and contributed to this book in ways they perhaps didn't even realize. There are many more people I could thank, but time, space, and modesty compel me to stop here.

FOREWORD

When we meet someone who has a transformed life, they always seem more interesting and more engaging. They have a renewed energy, they are passionate about their work, about life and in general about everything.

Would you like to learn more about how to lay a robust and solid foundation for building long-term wealth for you and your unborn generation?

Have you ever thought about your life purpose and doing the work you were created and called to do, where you enter a role that frees you to utilize 100% of your gifts, talents, and acquired skills?

Have you ever thought about how to convert your idea to a new venture and everything else in between, like building a learning organization, product creation, effective partnership, sphere mastery, leading from the future, business model creation, creating systems, strategy and more?

In this book, you will find simple ideas, patterns, guidelines and suggestions that you can follow, to empower you to transform your life, wealth and legacy for you and your lineage.

"Chukwudi is someone who has definitely overcome many life-changing events and found a way into on-going transformation. When you hear him speak you know there is something different, something resonates; what he is saying is true, even though you may not have heard it expressed in that way before. His vision is a world where everyone is living their life purpose and moving towards an extraordinary life; he seeks a Worldwide Wealth Reformation to address systemic poverty and exploitation. I'm sure there are many ideas and suggestions in this book that will resonate with you."

Raymond Aaron

(Leading Transformational Success Mentor and New York Times Best-Selling Author)

A NOTE FROM THE AUTHOR

Wealthyaire: How to Build Economic Endurance is not only special to me but also invigorating and open for further discourse among people who won't settle for less. It is an expression of a blend of experiences drawn from my years of interacting with different cultures, geographical space, spiritual and intellectual dialogues. I have seen lives changed, emotions shifted, energies aligned and wealth created. By studying the bible, the life of Christ and working with and interviewing some of the worlds' most successful and high-performing people, I discovered a proven blueprint that is used by top entrepreneurs, business owners and leaders to scale up their life and wealth, and which I have distilled in this book.

This book has already inspired many people to move forward in their lives, in ways they previously never thought possible. The breakthroughs we've witnessed are already AMAZING. You are part of a Worldwide Wealth Reformation to address systemic poverty and exploitation - amazing things have only just begun.

Wealthyaire: How to Build Economic Endurance is the first book in the Wealthyaire series. The next book is Leverage. Leverage compliments and builds on the Wealthyaire book. When you read this book, I know you are going to want to give it to your friends, family and loved ones. You are going to want to make sure your local libraries have it, and that every book charity has it in their inventory to distribute to their clients. In a word, I want YOU to become part of the Wealth Reformation! I am going to give you bonuses when you access www.wealthyaire.com/bonuses

CONTENTS

PART ONE: THE FUNDAMENTALS

These two things constantly reveal who we are and what we stand for; *events* and *interpretation of events*. Sometimes people take a miracle like a suspense of a natural law and try to explain it away. Whatever way we look at it, there are laws and principles that when we follow and pursue, sustained breakthrough and an opening up of our extraordinary future will be the outcome.

In all of human history three things have transformed society more than anything else:

1. Violence;

2. Knowledge;

3. Wealth.

The greatest of these is wealth; wealth is an outcome of what we do daily. To create and sustain it, we need to be people that cross over to the unfamiliar at every session; this requires the ability to continuously renew our minds, reconciling our past, understanding our tribe, accelerating into our future, embracing abundance and honouring the supernatural invitation; something far greater than working harder. My prayer is that you would find keys and building blocks in this manuscript that would unlock your legacy, transform your life and release prosperity on your children's children. May it be on earth as it in heaven!

MACRO PROSPERITY

We all have our individual prosperity within national and international economies. However national prosperity needs to be anchored on pillars such as Constitutional Freedom, Economic Sensibility, Government by the People, Honest Foreign Relations and Citizen Responsibility.

Constitutional Freedom

- Individuals have rights superior to all levels of government - citizens are not subjects, and birth is not destiny.
- States have reserved rights over the federal government.
- The 10 Commandments will be the fundamental ingredient for the code of morality and justice for all.

The purpose of the Constitution is to provide and maintain the rule of law, due process, independent courts, free and independent press, and transparency.

Economic Sensibility

- Government debt should never exceed 70% of GDP - optimum debt would be 50% of GDP.
- No more than 10% of the population should depend on the government for direct primary support.
- 90% of the population should pay some minimal amount of tax or contribute to the national treasury, even if their income is from welfare support.

Government by the People

- The city is the primary unit of political authority. States are made up of cities. The nation, as a federation, is made up of states.
- Localism, including churches, is critical to meeting society's needs.

The government's purpose is to implement policies that meet society's priorities, based on proven principles.

Honest relations anchored on*:*

- Rule of law;
- Due process;
- Independent courts;
- Free and independent press;
- Transparency (including a Freedom of Information Act)

These five axioms are what nations should be promoting to help foster governments' prosperity and build a positive relationship with our foreign partners. Therefore, the purpose of foreign policy is to establish these five principles worldwide.

Citizen's Responsibility

Citizens have an obligation to contribute as much as they take from society to the best of their ability. That way, we hold each other accountable for our determinations based upon principles that bind us. We need to take time to determine for ourselves, as citizens, what eternal truths we believe and want to pass on to the next generation as their inheritance of values.

Effective Macros

Build partnerships that will facilitate:

- Skills upgrade and continuous development;
- Infrastructure improvement and Investment;
- Stronger people-to-people ties;
- Developmental assistance.

An example of this type of partnership is the Asia-Africa Growth Corridor (AAGC). *AAGC* was conceived in November 2016; it is an economic cooperation agreement between the governments of India and Japan, which offers an ambitious reboot of their long-standing economic and development ties with the African continent. The scheme promises to open up a new era of cooperation, with a refreshed impetus to efforts long overshadowed by the hyperactive role of China in Africa.

An AAGC vision document was created in May 2017 based on consultations with Asian and African think-tanks. It aims for Indo-Japanese collaboration to develop quality infrastructure in Africa, complemented by digital connectivity, which would undertake the realization of the idea of creating a free and open Indo-Pacific Region.

WEALTH, MICRO PROSPERITY AND MONEY

WEALTH

When I mention wealth, I don't necessarily mean money and more importantly – I mean the many intangible things money cannot buy. Wealth is a "more than enough" mind-set, a "nothing is impossible" belief system, light in the darkness, wholeness in brokenness, beauty for ashes, oil of gladness instead of mourning and a "can-do" attitude. Wealth is an ability to create positives outcomes in the midst of lack and emptiness through wisdom and strength. True wealth is first a condition of the heart that influences the world around you.

When we contract the difference between rich mind-sets and wealth mind-sets. Most rich people think their money protects them, even from the law. Solomon put it like this: The rich, in their conceit, imagine that their wealth is enough to protect them. It becomes their confidence in a day of trouble. (Proverbs 18:11 THT). Wealthy people are humble, as they are thankful, knowing their source is the Lord. Rich people think of their assets, wealthy people dream of their legacy. The rich person's business goal is to make money, while a wealthy person's vocation brings profit as the fruit of serving others well. These contracts are a few examples to illustrate how people in each mind-set think. They help explain why many people that are rich, a fewer number of them are wealthy.

True wealth is based on the generosity of your soul, not just on your positive personal outlook, family lineage or your level of intelligence. Every believer is summoned to be generous. When you give to God, He gives back to you thirty, sixty, hundred and a thousand times more. If it is true that you cannot out-give God, then it stands to reason that all believers are called to be wealthy. He who is faithful in a very little thing is faithful also in much; and he who is unrighteous in a very little thing is unrighteous also in much. (Luke 16:10 NASB).

Economic endurance can be sustained through wealth creation when business is done supernaturally. God has the science of wealth and success all figured out; we need to press in and show up daily. When we show up God can show off and He can exhibit himself. Wealth is generally misunderstood; wealth comes in multiple forms. And you are anointed for the transfer of wealth. Because you see, as the seed of Abraham, it's ingrained in your very DNA. To be able to get and create wealth. I am talking about 'the God-given power to manifest or create out of nothing; something that has the ability to manifest resources that previously did not exist'.

The wealth ladder below is my perspective of various wealth building blocks and their level of value.

Wealth Ladder

Utmost Value| True riches: Integrity, Shalom, Joy, Identity, Rest, Salvation

Secondary Value| Skills and Experience

Tertiary Value| Position and Influence

Lowest Value | Money

What are the different dimensions of wealth that exist out there? Let's think about various ways wealth can be generated:

- Wealth of access;
- Wealth of assets;
- Wealth of creativity;
- Wealth of ability.

You could have the wealth of access, one or two people away from the person that you need to form the synergy required to advance; this synergy will yield an amplification of the power to generate wealth, however access to the Secret Place of the Most High, the realm where God is real and He shares His secrets, is the greatest form of access.

We live in shifting times where our rate of learning has to be ahead of the rate of change for us to keep translating creativity into assets. Your money is in the idea; I mean the idea that is in demand or a weakness in the existing competition.

Wealth creation requires you to be a pioneer. The dictionary defines a pioneer as *"someone who explores, prepares or opens up a new way; someone who takes the lead or initiative"*. Pioneers are found in every area of life, including religion. The wealth pioneer's various seasons of life need to be in proximity to the right people because the wealth isn't just the idea, the wealth is partly their tribe coming into unity for the synergy of the ages.

In Ancient Egypt, when Pharaoh had his two dreams (Genesis chapter 41), he wasn't short of interpretations and meanings. "Pharaoh sent and called all the necromancers of Egypt and all its sages, and related to them his dream, but no one interpreted them for Pharaoh. Meaning, not one of them offered an interpretation which satisfied Pharaoh until Joseph (1557-1447 BC) came along and offered his divinely inspired interpretation.

The seven fat cows and healthy ears represented seven years of plenty; the skinny cows with beaten ears represented seven years of extreme famine. The same thing occurred in the second dream where he saw the skinny beaten ears together with the healthy ones. Joseph then continued to give his advice on what should be done and in so doing he clarified everything.

In other words, Pharaoh respected his knowledge, understanding, wisdom and economic intelligence – otherwise, he would not have raised Joseph to a position of power. Joseph was on exhibition in order to solve a problem that nobody else could solve so that a platform of credibility would be established for the sharing of his faith and economic intelligence. Joseph built silos to capture a harvest because he had the interpretation of what to do. God wants us to create silos for the transformation of earth and the silos are built out of the relationships that come together. What fills the relationships is the unique form of wealth that is going to be manifested through your tribe.

Your relationships will create the silos into which wealth gets transferred in the coming season.

One of the primary activities of angels (angel network) is the acquisition or creation of wealth or in the advancement of heaven's agenda on earth; this involves putting you at the right place at the right time to meet the right person for the right exchange of an idea or concept. In other words, one of your secret weapons is the capacity to meet the right person at the right time. Relationships are vehicles that advance your wealth and the body of Christ. You need to be open to those new relationships.

Wealth is for the bold and empowered. One fundamental vehicle of getting to a place of empowerment for me is that I edify myself, by praying in tongues. One who speaks in a tongue edifies himself (1 Corinthians 14:4). Now the word for edify is edifice. I pray in a private "prayer language" through the Holy Ghost so that I keep building an edifice to house the revelation of the mind of Christ; this enables me to house the anointing that is missing in my life and to house a container for a genius insight.

Since Christ is the source of all knowledge, understanding, wisdom, authority, power, glory and majesty (every other source is an echo or a counterfeit), when I access the mind of Christ, it's beyond my mind. However, I have authorised access by my own utterance, I pray into manifestation what was pre-scripted of me in the womb by God before time began. This type of access when stewarded well, in my opinion, gives us access to the greatest form of wealth. Access to the right "somebody" is crucial in equipping you and creating the synergy required. You only need to have a divine appointment with one person and you can ramp up. This is what I'm saying, 'think of yourself as a participant in the transfer of wealth that is in the earth, to solve a problem that no one else can solve'.

Would you like to see how this works? That was what Jesus did. When he went throughout Israel, he healed the sick and cast out devils. Most of us miss the point. It wasn't that you're supposed to be focusing and copying only his Messianic healing deliverance ministry. It was that when he showed up, he got results no one could get, addressing the problem no one else could solve. His problem-solving and solution-driven life has been unparalleled. No one has been able to achieve such feats!

Start thinking about the systemic issues of society that are supposed to be solved and what are the supernatural problem-solving abilities you've got for a problem, which the world can't solve, and that it is looking for an answer to and can't get. That's where you are expected to show up. See, God gives you the power to create wealth; you don't have to get someone else's wealth. You don't have to take over the company; you can create what doesn't exist. That's the power that is in you inherently in the Abrahamic covenant. The catch is wealth comes in different forms and it's not just in money. When wealth is manifesting through creativity, you've got to learn how to translate your creativity into assets and assets that adapt as they produce value. Your money isn't the money; your money is the idea and concepts.

To build economic endurance you have to be either a business owner or an investor or both, or a professional who is investing in a machine that creates wealth. When you make money as a professional, the problem is that you are the income source and if you stop working the bills starts mounting. I love integrity, identity and the rest, but you can have them all and still be broke.

There are many factors that translate into your wealth; they include your vision, market, calling, stewardship, partnerships, and sometimes the great continuum takes a turn you don't expect.

MONEY

Money is a type of asset in an economy that is used to buy goods and services from people and organizations.

Money provides:

1. A means of payment (medium of exchange);
2. A unit of account;
3. A store of value.

The types of money that have been used in the past century include:

1. Commodity money;
2. Representative money;
3. Fiat money;
4. Electronic Money;
5. Spiritual money.

The instrument or commodity used as money needs to satisfy the characteristics of money to gain widespread use. The commodity must be divisible into standardized quantities so that different units of value can be created. It must be durable so that it lasts; otherwise, it wouldn't function well as a store of value and it would have to be continually replaced. Small size and light weight are desirable for easy transport.

1. Commodity money: This is money whose value comes from the commodity of which it is made. Commodity money consists of objects that have value in them as well as value in their use as money. Commodity money has intrinsic value because of the type of material with which it is made and is valuable when not used as money. It has the ability to trade-in for valuable goods. In times of economic turmoil, such as severe economic depressions or hyperinflation, people sometimes turn to commodity money instead of the money authorized by their governments.

2. Representative money: This is a certificate or token which can be exchanged for the underlying commodity, but only as the trade is good for that source and the product. According to economist William Stanley Jevons (1875), representative money arose because metal coins often were "variously clipped or depreciated" during use, but using representations for the value stored in banks ensured its worth. He noted that paper and other materials have been used as representative money. In 1934 economist William Howard Steiner wrote that the term was used "at one time to signify that a certain amount of bullion was stored in the Treasury while the equivalent paper in circulation" represented the bullion.

3. Fiat money: Fiat money is printed money that only has value because the government says so. Its value is not based on gold; it has no intrinsic value. A recent example is when the Indian government eliminated 500 and 1,000-rupee paper notes from its financial system. The alteration occurred essentially overnight. Indian Prime Minister Narendra Modi initiated the policy on Nov. 8th, 2016, and

the shock caused bank closures across the country. The banned currency had accounted for nearly 80% of the total outstanding notes in circulation throughout the Indian economy.

4. Electronic money: Money exists mainly in electronic format today, as records in the databases of financial institutions. This is one reason why the United States Treasury no longer prints currency in denominations greater than $100. Law-abiding citizens use checks or electronic transfers for large payments, while organized crime and terrorist networks prefer cash. Consequently, the elimination of large denomination bills is considered a potent weapon against organized crime and terrorists, by making it inconvenient and risky to transfer large amounts of cash. The European Central Bank has permanently stopped the production of the 500-euro note.

5. Spiritual money: Robert Kiyosaki, author of the "The Rich Dad, Poor Dad" series of books, mentioned that after looking at much research on four kinds of money, he came to the conclusion that there is a fifth kind of money that he had never seen before. He called it "spiritual money." He didn't have a grid for it until he started working with non-profit organizations and foundations and found they operated on a totally different set of blueprints to anything he had ever worked with for personal and business wealth acquisition. Somehow, the non-profits reviewed were aligning with a cause that was so unearthly that Kiyosaki's only deduction was that God must be supernaturally resourcing those organizations. Essentially, Heaven was in the assignment and drew the resources in.

Rabbi Daniel Lapin put it this way, 'Money is simply a certificate of appreciation for the value you have given'. Money or value can exchange hands in one of two ways, by choice or by force. If I do not willingly trade my value with you and you take it from me, you are taking my life, you are stealing from me, you are violating my life.

When your labour is involved in producing a service or product, because your labour went into producing it, it is now yours - I understand that your labour

WEALTHYAIRE: HOW TO BUILD ECONOMIC ENDURANCE   19

is an extension of your life and person, meaning when you worked you have to expend time on a task, whatever you produced from that task will not have existed without your labour. You have an investment in it. What I am saying is that your money is your life.

Joe Dominguez, et al in his book 'Your Money, Your Life', brings home the real cost of your job or charity on your life; it enables the reader to put money and work vastly into perspective. The table that lists how much *life energy hours* are left from a certain age is especially moving.

The ancient world worked on the barter system, where they traded their labour and pieces of their life with each other. If someone cultivated an apple tree, harvested apples but wanted lamb meat, they gave up that little piece of life they invested in apples, to get the meat they needed. It would be a fair trade because the apple farmer already had too many apples.

This can work well in a small village but does not scale with more complex needs. Fortunately, humans figured out they could trade their products and services for one common commodity they all chose to value for exchange and this became known as a trade medium. Today we have paper money; which originated from a banknote, where the piece of paper represented a portion of gold. The Dutch started this approach of representing gold with paper. The original dollar bill represented 1 twentieth of an ounce of gold. Today gold is over 1,300 USD an ounce. A one-dollar bill will have been worth so much more if it was still tied to 1 twentieth of an ounce of gold. Most countries went off their precious mental standard in the last century. Most countries use paper money with no backing.

Money is something that everyone can trade their labour in for if we agree on the unit. It does not really matter except if your currency and the countries that own it has Special Drawing Rights (SDR) interest within the IMF. Likewise, what gives gold its value is that we have decided it is valuable.

When we are using money and we are trading our apples as an example, each unit of money has a fixed market value and this can lead some people to the zero-sum game, where they imagine that there is only so much money in the world, and they all have some form of value - so only so many people can have some of these pounds. The problem with this argument is that a pound does not have a set value; we may think that it kind of has a value, but when I am at the marketplace with my products or services, like a barrel of apples, and someone says, "Can I buy your barrel of apple for twenty pounds?", I have to make a decision internally. Is the time and energy I put into making the barrel of apples worth twenty pounds? If I think it is worth more, I may haggle and if the person does not want to trade with me they may go somewhere else. I determine the value of the apples or whatever my products may be, thus the value of the pounds or dollars. This means each set of pounds has no value because it is only determined by people who are trading with each other.

It really comes down to the value of the fruit of my labour.

If we decide how much our labour is worth, then money does not exist. Wow! Think of it - if there is no actual value in the little piece of white and brown paper, the only value is that we as a society have decided this can represent our labour. As that can change from transaction to transaction, how can that be anything tangible in the world? This means that ultimately there is no money - only your mind. If we go back to the zero-sum game thought, where for some to be rich others have to be poor, then now that does not exist, because there is actually no limit to the value you can ascribe to a twenty-pound note. What exists is our labour and the wealth we create with it, like the cloth we make, the machine we think up, develop and build. What exists is what we create.

Some people only get money by taking it; here I am talking about creating value. This requires a continuous shift in the way we think about value and wealth. Most of the ancient world operated feudal societies, where the way a nation got wealth was that they either exploited their people, or conquered other territories or nations, and exploited these people. In fair capitalism, you become wealthy by serving your fellow man. Getting wealthy in a free market economy means that you served your fellow man well; in capitalism, I am producing value and I am trading it on the market.

Most people need the permission to prosper because they have inner conflicts. We live in a world where some people do not have permission to prosper because they believe there is not enough for everyone or that money is evil. You will have probably heard the phrase "money is the root of all evil." The culture in the West is awash with messages that prosperity is wrong and that the highest moral standard that anyone can live by is that they don't do anything for themselves, always for the good of others and society. Some are taught that money is evil, while others are taught that for someone to be rich others have to be poor. This makes their desire to prosper evil. *Money can't be evil - to say that money is evil is to call people's work and labour evil.* That means that any creativity that people find valuable is evil. This is wrong. It leads to bad things and oppressed people. Desiring a lot of money is not evil as long as you are financially ethical about your business.

> *"But those who [are not financially ethical and] crave to get rich [with a compulsive, greedy, longing for wealth] fall into temptation and a trap and into many foolish and harmful desires that plunge people into ruin and destruction [leading to personal misery]. For the love of money [that is, the greedy desire for it and the willingness to gain it unethically] is a root of all sorts of evil, and some by longing for it have wandered away from the faith and pierced themselves [through and through] with many sorrows."* (1 Timothy 6:9-10 Amplified Bible)

The scripture here shows that the love of money is a root of many evils and not the root of every kind of evil, if you don't understand where money comes from, what it is, and that it represents value and labour of people, and you love material possessions more than you love people, you can, and most likely will, commit all kinds of evil things to get it. I subscribe to the universal principles of nature; I believe these principles were set in motion by God. When we understand the philosophical framework for money and prosperity, by going back into the spiritual, it will erase internal conflicts.

To be rich means you have produced a lot of value for a lot of people.

The full value of our life cannot be represented or transmitted by money; not all of the values in your life can be monetized. Your bank account does not equal your wealth. The value of your friendship, the value of the love you show and so many things that consist of our lives and our value cannot be monetized. I know people who have huge amounts of money but I consider them to be poor.

Money represents the value that others have traded for, the value you can or have traded with other people, and it is just a piece of the overall eternal value we have as humans.

Money is not a zero-sum game - meaning for someone to be rich somebody else has to be poor; the equation does not equal zero. Money is good and it merely represents what you do, what your labour has produced. Money also represents your products and services and it can be translated into something we can all exchange. We trade value for value; this means that wealth is unlimited if what we are really trading is value. There is no limit to it. For one to be rich you don't have to take money from someone else. The main thing holding back global prosperity is a type of mind-set. The fact is, there are enough money, food, land, water and raw materials for the world. We have no shortage of resources. The rich want to spread the resources, because the more the resources spread, the more they can create and produce. Of course, there are some dubious business people that don't want the resources to spread. But for the most part business people are creators and they like creating - the more creators there are that they can partner with, the more fun they have.

I believe true entrepreneurship is very God-like. I will say apostolic, which means seeing the blueprint of heaven and bringing it down to earth. The apostolic sees the will of God and converts it to a tangible reality in the world around them for the benefit of mankind. The idea of being God-like, like an apostle, is to see something that does not exist in the world and then create it, make it into a reality. This is what entrepreneurs do. We have a business idea; we expend our labour to create. If we think of some of the great examples in the business world like Henry Ford and Steve Jobs, they were the same way - they had these ideas they turned into reality and they changed the world because of it.

Money is good, it is not neutral. Some people teach and believe that money is amoral, that it is neutral; you could use money to do evil that is using other people's creativity and labour or your own to do evil. That is just evil, but it does not make money evil. Money is good. Wealth is unlimited because we create it, and there is no limit to the wealth.

The power to change the world rests in the hands of traders, not traitors, business people, entrepreneurs, those people that are creating massive wealth through adding value; they are the ones changing the world. You have permission to prosper, you can prosper with purpose. One of the requirements to change the world, among others, is not just having permission to prosper, but also a mandate to prosper.

Learn to love time more than money. Money is a tool to buy back our greatest commodity – time. You can get money back but not time.

In his books, Rickards, J. (2015) The Death of Money: The Coming Collapse of the International Monetary System Paperback. James stated that today's international monetary system is largely based on the U.S. dollar. James suggest that a new collapse could be triggered by a loss of confidence in the dollar and its role as a store of value. This would have a knock-on effect on the euro and sterling too. Based on the monetary history of the past century, collapses have not meant the end of the world. Instead, monetary collapse meant that the major financial and trading powers of the time sat down around the table and rewrote the rules of the game.

PROSPERITY

Prosperity is simply having enough of God's provisions to complete his instructions in your life. Prosperity increases your ability to bless others. Prosperity is not a miracle. It is the divine reward for honouring a divine law. To increase in prosperity, we need to look for problems to solve. Every problem is a potential business. Everything God has made is a solution to a problem. Your economic worth and significance are determined by the kinds of problems you are solving for someone. If you want to earn £100 an hour, you must find a £100-an-hour problem to solve. Your significance is not your similarity to others. It is your difference. It is essential you find your point of difference and solve a problem with it.

Your worth is determined by the kinds of problems you are willing to solve for someone.

Find someone else in trouble. Mechanics solve car problems and lawyers solve legal problems. Doctors solve physical or health problems. You are a walking solution for someone in trouble. Find out who is in trouble and provide a solution for them, then Prosperity will be inevitable for you. God has been speaking of BREAKTHROUGH! God doesn't want to just break you through; He wants to keep you through. He is breaking old cycles that have hindered your life. It's no longer breakthrough to crises. It's breakthrough to breakthrough. Glory to glory! Embrace true prosperity.

As a six-year-old, I learned the Lord's Prayer and the phrase, "Lead us not into temptation", and it has had a very strong impression on me. What does this really mean? We are all praying for growth, increase, asset, and taking territory. Nobody ever prays, 'And keep me from prosperity and success beyond my capacity to handle.' But, that's one thing the Lord's Prayer is covering when it states: "keep us from temptation." The translation could be: "Lead us not into a situation that we succeed to the point where our vulnerabilities are exploited and we end up getting taken out." Maybe that's why most people don't have the wealth that they hear prophesied to them, or the influence and all that goes along with it. Essentially, whatever homework isn't done on the personal mountain, shows up in the career mountain. This is especially true if you are a believer contending for new territory in career convergence.

Our economic status shapes our perceptions and expectations, and that really influences choices and actions. People in poverty face challenges virtually unknown to those in the middle class or upper class - challenges from both obvious and hidden sources. The reality of being poor brings, out a survival mentality, and turns attention away from opportunities taken for granted by everyone else. There are "hidden rules" among classes. If you work with people from poverty, some understanding of how different their world is from yours will be invaluable. Payne, R. K. (2013) A Framework for Understanding Poverty; A Cognitive Approach 5th Edition can help in this regard. The table below is a study of patterns, not stereotypes. All patterns have exceptions. Poverty occurs in all races and all countries. Poverty has systemic and exploitation causes and poverty is also caused by thinking, individual choices, mind-set, addiction, illness, war, lack of education and lack of employment. Poverty is as much about intergenerational transfer of knowledge, as it is about money and social class.

Hidden Rules Among Classes

Item	Poverty	Middle-Class	Wealthy Class
Possessions	People	Things	One-of-a-kind objects, legacies, pedigrees
Money	To be used, spent	To be managed	To be conserved, invested
Personality	Is for entertainment; sense of humour is highly valued	Is for acquisition and stability; achievement is highly valued	Is for connections; financial, political, social connections are highly valued
Food	Key question: Did you have enough? Quantity most important	Key question: Did you like it? Quality most important	Key question: Was it presented well? Presentation most important
Time	Present most important; decisions made for moment based on feelings or survival	Future most important; decisions made against future ramifications.	Traditions and history most important; decisions made partially on basis of tradition and decorum.
Family Structure	Tends to be matriarchal	Tends to be patriarchal	Whoever has the Money or Anointing
Language	Casual register; language is about survival	Formal register; language is about negotiation	Formal register; language is about networking

Item	Poverty	Middle-Class	Wealthy Class
Love	Love and acceptance conditional, based on whether individual is liked	Love and acceptance conditional and based on largely on achievement	Love and acceptance conditional and related to social standing and connections
Humour	About people	About situations	About social faux pas
Worldview	Sees world in terms local setting	Sees world in terms national setting	Sees world in terms international setting
Driving forces	Survival, relationships, entertainment	Work, achievement	Financial, political, social connections
Destiny	Believes in fate; powerless to change much	Believes in choice; power to change future with good decisions	Noblesse and oblige

A Framework for Understanding Poverty (Ruby K. Payne (Year2013)

"And God blessed them and said to them, be fruitful, multiply, and fill the earth, and subdue it [using all its vast resources in the service of God and man]; and have dominion over the fish of the sea, the birds of the air, and over every living creature that moves upon the earth." (Genesis 1:28 Amplified Bible)

The command to have dominion (govern, rule, manage, control) has been given to all men. To be fruitful means to be productive, to produce something. To multiply means to reproduce your products and services in bulk. To fill the earth means to distribute; it deals with distribution networks and channels so your goods and services get to all the earth. To subdue means to control the market. To have dominion you need to be fruitful, multiply, fill the earth and subdue. From this Bible verse (Genesis 1:28), *Dominion is a result, not a pursuit, and poverty can be summed up as the absence of self-production.* The poor are not those who lack, it is the non-productive ones - this can be due to numbers of factors like a poverty trap, poverty spirit (the lies you tell yourself and come into agreement with), mind-set (conscious and subconscious), generational thinking, and lack of wisdom and creativity.

Prospering in Any Economy

In the realm of building wealth through a business, it takes a lot of work and effort to make things look effortless or seamless - it takes a lot of work to get "effortless" success. Below, is an approach to creating a product or service, that people will pay for, in any economy:

1. Find your tribe;
2. Build a community;
3. Listen to what your community is saying as it relates to your area of speciality to see where you can help. Listen to what they are complaining about;
4. Build the product or service;
5. Sell them the thing they want.

In the Hebrew of Scripture, there's no true verb for 'to have.' There's no real or exact way of saying 'I have.' Essentially in divine tongue, we can't possess anything of this world. The house you bought is an illusion, if it was really yours, you could keep it. But you can't keep anything of this world. Everything you have is temporary, and in the end, you have to let everything go. What you think you have is only entrusted or borrowed.

> *"But godliness actually is a source of great gain when accompanied by contentment [that contentment which comes from a sense of inner confidence based on the sufficiency of God]. For we have brought nothing into the world, so [it is clear that] we cannot take anything out of it, either."* (1 Timothy 6:6-7 Amplified Bible)

When you think you have what you don't have, you live in conflict with the truth. In order to live in the truth, you have to live in "no have'". "Yes, to live with 'no have.' And if you don't have, then you can't have any problems or worries. They will be out there, but you don't have them. You can't even be burdened down by the weight of your own life because you don't have your life or its burdens. Now not everything is temporary, the one thing you can have is God. God is the only true possession. And it's only when you let go of all that you don't have, that you can be free to have Him. We need to learn the secret of living with "no have" and possess God.

PURPOSE

Your purpose is what you were created for, it is connected to your identity, your identity lays the foundation for your purpose to be actualized. Through the ages, people have been asking the questions of 'Who am I?', 'Where do I can from?', and 'What is my purpose?'. Identity is knowing who you are and your best self. Your identity changes what you see, this makes it easier for you to know what to say 'no' or 'yes' to. Identity is also connected to *mission*. Your mission is typically connected to who you impact and who you serve.

When you are clear about who you are and who you serve, your identity and your mission will lead you through several contradictions until you come to a place of convergence. The people that you're going to impact and whose lives are going to be affected by your existence will then carry the footprint of your legacy. Life is a gift and the giver is good; everybody is created in the image of God.

If you are not clear about your purpose, then you can look to do something that meets a need that may be monetized. As you carry on in your journey, realise that no experience is wasted, even if you don't like what you are currently doing. It is all part of the preparation, testing and trial you need to pass; remember the tests of servant-hood, humility and character are required for every shift.

To accelerate your purpose, *utterance* is a powerful thing, especially when decreeing and declaring who you are. Most times you have to have a statement written that says, for example, "This is my abridged purpose: "To lay a foundation to eliminate systemic poverty in Africa through education and supernatural business".

People on the path of purpose don't have time for drama, because for them the bigger mission washes away all the silliness; instead of complaining they just honour the process or struggle required to succeed. Their dream is bigger than the thing you can complain about.

I have asked questions personally at various times to gain clarity with regards to purpose. Yet to us God has unveiled and revealed them by and through His

Spirit, for the [Holy] Spirit searches diligently, exploring and examining every-thing, even sounding the profound and bottomless things of God [the divine counsels and things hidden and beyond man's scrutiny] (1 Corinthians 2:10 Amplified Bible)

    a. Holy Ghost, show me what was written in God's book concerning me before the creation of the earth?

    b. Father, I want you to share with me your secrets and when you see me show me what you see?

    c. Father, what are your thoughts concerning me, what is in your heart and what do you want to see in my life right now that is not there?

    d. Lord, what are you doing in this region and what is my role in it?

    e. Lord, show me what I am meant to be doing for the rest of my life?

    f. Holy Spirit, show me what I should be doing right now to lead from the future?

    g. Holy Spirit, what are the unique patterns I am to manifest as a son of God?

    h. Holy Spirit, show me where I am falling into the trap of false comparison?

Obviously, the caveat to asking the types of questions above is that you need to be able to hear the voice and thoughts of the Holy Spirit in various ways after you have built a relationship with Him.

If you can't ask the Holy Spirit questions then you can start by answering the questions below. This may help you zero down on your work or your job. You may initially come up with answers that do not resonate with your spirit. Elim-inate such answers and try again to get answers that resonate.

    a. What do I see?

    b. What do I want?

    c. What do I desire?

    d. What matters to me?

    e. What will I do for the rest of my life if money was not an issue?

    f. What will I do for the rest of my life that will give me enough juice?

g. Does it excite me?

h. Why have I not started the answer to question "d, e and f"?

i. How do I feel now that I am here?

j. How do I think now that I am here?

Your PURPOSE drives your MISSION.

Everybody in the world has something that excites them. When you can get clear on your purpose and begin to declare it, then you start to reprogram your mind to who you really are. Otherwise, your brain may have had a whole lot of toxic scripting and programming that will struggle to interfere with your declarations.

Ultimately purpose involves being in a flow where you are working in a rhythm of destiny that God wrote for your life before you were born. This involves being in a place where everything seems to be flowing as though it was pre-scripted and you were experiencing divine appointments that were set up before you got to the space-time. When you hit that rhythm, you are hitting a field of research called the "convergence zone".

The convergence zone is when you step into the work that God prepared for you to fulfil before you were born. When you are in the convergence zone everything that you need to succeed has already been factored into the environment. What is crucial sometimes is for you to speed up or press in. God will always put us in proximity to destiny, our role is recognition and focusing on the opportunities so we can pursue and overtake. Waiting for it to come to us is not a strategy and will not work.

When you get into your divine purpose, that is the thing that you were created to do; you are not innovating something. You aren't originating something. You are discovering that which was already scripted and written for you to enter into. In other words, you're entering into the script that was already written.

Your calling is the system, process, agenda, circumstance, scenario, activity or events by which God reveals to you your purpose, this happens when pre-destination and fore-knowing collide. God fore-knew you before you were born, you were called to God before the foundation of the world, God thought of you and related with you before you existed in your physical form and he separated a piece of himself and kept you in Himself - that part of you was watching as God wrote all the days of your life in his Book.

> *"My frame was not hidden from you, when I was made in secret, and skilfully wrought in the depths of the earth; Your eyes have seen my un-formed substance; and in your book were all written the days that were ordained for me, when as yet there was not one of them. How precious also are your thoughts to me, O God! How vast is the sum of them."* (Psalm 139:15-17 New American Standard Bible)

When you serve from the point of your true Identity, not under the labels others have put on you, you can access the full blessings of a son or daughter. When you know who you truly are, in the context of God's purpose for you, you will become unstoppable as obstacles become stepping stones.

You are authorized.

The stage is set. You can feel the warmth of the spotlights on your face. You can hear the audience quieting down now. You are mere moments away from the curtain rising and stepping into the performance of a lifetime. God has written a script for you. It's the perfect script. It's your destiny. When you follow His script, you walk in the area of your purpose and power is released! God meets you there and anoints you to usher in Heaven to earth. When you step up God shows off.

Our existence is a love story, where the bride is a picture of what we were created to be. We were created to be the bride and can never be complete by ourselves. That is why deep down in the centre of our being, in the deepest part of our heart we seek to be filled. For the bride is made to be married. We can never find our completion until we are joined to Him who is beyond us. This is why we go through life trying to join ourselves; to join ourselves to that which we think will fill the longing of our heart. We join ourselves to people, success, achievements, possessions, comfort, money, acceptance, romance, beauty, power, family, a movement, a goal, and any multitude of things. The bride was created to be married and she can never rest until she is. The bridegroom is God, the one for whom we were created. A bride marries the bridegroom, we need to marry God by joining every part of our being to Him, only then can we be complete, only then can our deepest longing be fulfilled. The mystery of our heart is the mystery of the bride. The bride can only find her completion in the bridegroom. The bridegroom of our soul is God.

VISION AND VISION MAPPING

"For the vision is yet for an appointed time, but at the end it shall speak, and not lie: though it tarry, wait for it; because it will surely come, it will not tarry." (Habakkuk 2:3)

A vision is a picture of a preferred future state, a description of what it would be like at a point in time. It is a vibrant picture of the future. It is more than a dream or set of hopes; it is a commitment. The vision provides the context for designing or managing the changes that will be necessary to reach those goals.

A clear vision keeps you on course and on purpose. It forecasts the total journey you are about to take and gives you something to strive toward. It represents the higher purpose of your life or business, it is something to which you and your business aspire. Your vision needs to be so clear and focused that you will be proud to share it at will with every person you meet.

A business without a vision can be compared to a plane without a flight plan – the plane will wander aimlessly, never knowing where it will land or even refuel because of not having a destination. Most people have an impression of what they want to do - but that impression is not a vision. Your vision will chart your course and keep you true to what you want to achieve. *I encourage you to work on your vision with a team - so your limiting beliefs and history don't hinder the scope of your business or legacy.*

From a corporate perspective, Collins and Porras' book *Built to Last* (1997) states that visions required four things:

1. Purpose;

2. Mission;

3. Descriptive Narrative; and

4. Values.

Mission

The mission of a company is comprised of the big initiatives that you are going to accomplish. These are the mechanics or tangible steps your business will take to making your vision a reality. Your Mission Statement will consist of a list of goals and strategic actions that your business is striving to achieve – as you complete each of the goals and tasks you will check them off and revise the list.

Examples of Vision and Mission Statements

Airbus' vision statement: To create the best and safest aircraft.

Airbus' mission statement: To meet the needs of airlines and operators by producing the most modern and comprehensive aircraft family on the market, complemented by the highest standard of product support.

Airbus' Purpose: Airbus' long-term strategic purpose is expressed in its strategic company vision of 'creating the best and safest aircraft'. This very future-orientated and enduring message is even more confirmed by the mission statement, which follows the principle, as stated above.

Cisco's vision statement: Changing the Way We Work, Live, Play, and Learn.

Cisco's mission statement: Shape the future of the Internet by creating unprecedented value and opportunity for our customers, employees, investors, and ecosystem partners.

Cisco has seen a lot of growth and expansion in its over 30 years of existence. In this span of time, it has acquired several other brands whose number is more than 155. Its vision states no clear future position for the brand. This has not been a problem for Cisco as it has continued to grow and expand at an impressive rate; strategy and planning have played a very important role in this regard.

A business can revise their mission and vision statements to respond to changing market situations and customer demands; a shift becomes crucial when the business feels that it is drifting away from its goals.

Descriptive Narrative

The descriptive narrative consists of words that a) elicit emotions and b) paint a vivid picture. Your business descriptive narrative is the linking statements that, when combined with specific words, are designed to drive specific emotions and clearly identifies the business you desire to build.

To create a vision map, the vision mapping process is a useful approach - it is the lifelong know-how of expressing your dreams by defining the goals you must reach on the way to achieving those dreams, determining the steps you must take to reach your goals, and writing down the tasks you must complete to take each step.

The Vision Mapping process is a powerful engine that will provide all of the vigour you need to reach your most important dreams.

Steps for Vision Mapping

I learnt about Vision Mapping from one of my mentors Steven Scott, the steps are:

1. Write out clearly defined dream or vision with descriptions;

2. Translate the vision or dream into a set of specific goals;

3. Transform each goal into a set of specific steps;

4. Translate each complex step into a specific set of tasks;

5. Set completion dates for each task, step and goal listed in 2,3 and 4.

Take Action

Create your Vision Mapping Journal.

A Vision Mapping Journal comprises a lifelong companion that empowers your dreams and lends structure to extraordinary outcomes. As the years come and go, you will discard some dreams and add new ones. The goal of your journal is to provide a clear roadmap and schedule for achieving each of your most important short-term, long-term, and lifetime dreams. It's your map ... it's your life.

Take it seriously, but have fun with it. As you do, your Vision Mapping Journal becomes your path in a notebook.

Once you have converted your steps into specific tasks, you will have a detailed map to lead you from where you are right now to the achievement of your goals and dreams. You have successfully mapped your vision. Without taking this first step of faith, it will be nearly impossible for you to convert your dreams into reality. The steps and tasks in your vision map will need daily monthly, quarterly and yearly milestones within your chart pipeline (see the session on timing).

SPHERE MASTERY

Mastery comes down to distinctions and the ability to adjust yourself to different levels of anointing, so when you are going up to a higher place you have the required spirit, skill, self, state and influence. The distinction is anchored on 30, 60, 100, 1000-fold revelations, you get the revelation at the 30-fold, work it out at 60, and multiply its demonstration at 100 and 1000-fold.

It's amazing to me that there can be this much similarity in the human species and yet so much distinctiveness. It shows that if we were to do a DNA crime scene investigation now and we looked at your thumbprint or your fingerprint, everyone's fingerprint here is a unique expression of the individual. That speaks of the nature of the creator. Two characteristics of the God you're working with are infinite variableness (infinite originality), and infinite creativity among principles, patterns and manifestations that are all similar.

Every snowflake is different and yet they are all similar. Every leaf is different, but they are all similar. Every person here is similar, for if you go to the best hospital in the world, they basically can do an operation on any one of you because, underneath the skin, the heart's going to be the same no matter where you go around the world, and the internal organs, the eyes, the optics. Yet every one individual is completely unique. It reveals two characteristics of God.

Sphere mastery is a journey that encompasses the human spirit, skill, self-awareness, state management and influence.

Spirit: Man is made up of a spirit, soul and body. The earthly coat, which is perishing, has a use-by date (expiry date), but the soul and spirit of man are eternal. Your human spirit connects you to God. Your spiritual life is the foundation of your life, it holds things together. The human spirit is made up of the communion, conscious and wisdom. The river of life from the throne of grace flows through the communion parts of the spirit. If you want to know how to walk into a room so that when you show up, the environment is affected, you need to discern the sphere that God called you to so that when you show up, your spirit dominates. Your spirit, in this regard, is your aura, resilience, that 'special thing' called 'the anointing', that empowers you in the face of any situation.

The anointing is the supernatural ability that God put upon your life in order to fix something that's broken, heal something that is sick, straighten out a situation that's crooked or smooth out something that's rough. You have an anointing to fix the problems on planet earth in your sphere. Think about this - you have an anointing and gifts mix to fix the situation that was ordained for you.

Skill: Skill is the ability that comes from acumen and practices. It often requires training, and experience, to do well and is the result of focused education. We need to know specifically what we are called to do in each phase of our life and channel-focused education in that area. For most specialized skills that can be monetized through products and services, true mastery may require putting into over 10,000 hours - this mastery is the zone of unconscious competence and it burns up the myth of people just falling into something without creating something with skill. *However, skillset without mindset will leave you upset.*

State of 'Being': This is closely related to self-awareness. The state of 'being' connotes occupying the position of being in charge; operating at a level of control, where circumstances don't play 'poker' on your mind, you do not react to but respond to situations. This further draw distinction between 'matured men' and 'mere boys'. The number one disposition you have to have to be in the game at the level you're about to play is the ability to step outside of your state at any moment, become aware of your state in any moment and make a decision to enter an empowering state first, regardless of what's going on around you. You would have a whole different attitude towards what's going on in your life because you'd see that there's an invisible 'something' behind the visible manifestation. If you have that kind of philosophy, then you recognise that the first order of business you've got is to get yourself into a resourceful state. If you are a believer, the number one danger to you is a victim state because a victim state never gets out of its own state because it gets attached to the pain.

There are two primary conditions you can ever be in. You are in the condition of being resourceful or not resourceful, and they extend from two mentalities; these are 'victim' or 'responsible'. What are you responsible for? Your destiny. That's why your accountability at the judgement seat of Christ is the single most powerful incentive the Apostle Paul could give towards the kind of life he wanted to live and the kind of life he wanted other people to live.

Influence: The "Law of Attraction" is pretty popular these days with New Age. Some think the Law of Attraction is some kind of cosmic "juju" that attracts people and opportunities to you. In reality, favour is the attraction of God to you that releases influence through you, so that other people are inclined to like, trust or cooperate with you - in the assignment God gave you!

This favour isn't "earthly" - it's a God-given, supernatural force that magnetizes you! Are you ready to be a people magnet?! The internal backdrop of this phenomenon includes motivation and stewardship.

Motivation: What influence do you want to have? Is your intent to manipulate or to bless? You and I both know this to be true, that you can guide people into particular experiences and thoughts. You can structure the transaction to serve yourself. But that's a far cry from what God actually does. He desires for you to move in a spirit of favour and operate from a place of wanting to bless - instead of wanting to get something from other people.

> *"The word of God is living and active, sharper than any two-edged sword, piercing to the division of soul and of spirit, of joints and of marrow, and discerning the thoughts and intentions of the heart."* (Hebrews 4:12)

No matter how shrewd you think you are, there is One who weighs our motivations. Ask yourself, "Do I have the character to sustain the influence God has given me?"

Stewardship: The Lord wants to entrust increase to His people and He wants to entrust it in a way that doesn't destroy you when you get it. Remember that he who is faithful with little will be trusted with much - this includes your influence with those God has placed in your path (Luke 16:10). God desires for you to prosper in business and in relationships.

Favour is a form of currency with which you can form supercharged alliances, if stewarded properly. These alliances get you where you want to go, faster! One of the greatest gifts that you could ever receive is the gift of favour and the power of supernatural attraction. We need the supernatural favour of God in business, and we need to resist the opposite spirit, which is a spirit of manipulation.

Questions:

What is your own motivation when it comes to influence?

Is your heart in alignment with God's heart to bless you and others?

Some people will say that the Beatles and someone like Bill Gates just happened to be at the right place at the right time, but if you look at the story of the Beatles, while other bands were looking for some hour of practices per week, the Beatles played together 7 hours per day, 6 days a week for a year. All day long they played music together - imagine the skill that they learnt together, how to start and stop songs, what moved people. They put in 10,000 hours before they broke out.

Bill went to a high school where his parents and other parents of the kids in his high school were rich enough to buy the only terminal access from a high school to a college mainframe in the US. His high school had an exclusive access to one of the US top computers, and while the college students push through to get a couple of hours here and there and waited on the queue, instead of tiring out waiting, he programmed consistently on the Mainframe, all night long for several nights. He got 10,000 hours developing his skill. The results have become an unprecedented record in human history!

Self-Awareness: Self-awareness deals with understanding character attributes that make you unique and distinctive and also informs the way we interact with others. They cause us to be able to influence, relate to and manage people around us. Character skills can and should be developed. Like focusing on your strengths, focusing on your strength will take you further than always trying to bolster your weaknesses, discovering what matters most to you, and what is unique about you.

PASSION, DESIRE AND HONOUR

PASSION

Passion is the fuel that drives you toward your dreams. It is so powerful that it keeps on burning even after you have achieved your dreams. Most successful and very rich people keep on working long after they have banked more money than they and all of their children, grandchildren and great-grandchildren could ever spend, Why?

Why can't Steven Spielberg, with a net worth of more than $3 billion, pass up a good script to direct? Or why does Elon Musk show up to pursue an entrepreneurial vision every single day, regardless of how he's feeling physically or emotionally? The fact is they are all fuelled by an incredible passion for what they are doing. Not only does passion drive the world's most successful people professionally, it also drives people who are the most successful in their personal pursuits. In fact, without passion, it is impossible to be extraordinarily successful in any arena, personally or professionally.

Passion is NOT an inborn trait. Although some people and some personality types exhibit energy and enthusiasm almost from birth, passion itself is not an inborn trait, because true passion always has an objective that it is focused on. For Mother Theresa, it was bringing comfort to the dying; for Steven Spielberg, it is taking words on a page and turning it into a visual and emotional experience that makes an awesome impact on his audience; for Bill Cosby, it is hearing his audience laugh and seeing the joy in their eyes.

The Three Essential Ingredients of Passion

1. Vision: A clearly defined dream with a precise and detailed map or plan to achieve that dream within a defined amount of time.
2. Hope: A well-founded and confident expectation that a specific dream, goal, step, or task will be accomplished within a defined amount of time. It is also an earnest expectation of good.
3. Fulfilment: The inner joy and excitement that comes from achieving meaningful goals, steps, and tasks that reflect personal core values.

If you are lacking passion in any area of your life, then I guarantee that you are lacking vision, hope, fulfilment or all three.

Use the Vision Mapping process to clarify vision. Defining your dream in writing gives you a clear and precise vision. Converting that dream to specific goals, steps, and tasks give you a genuine hope of reaching that dream. Completing each targeted task, step, and goal brings satisfaction and fulfilment.

DESIRE

Heaven also notes the desires that come from your heart and weaves their fulfilments into your journey. I often used to stress out over "not missing" the priority of God, never realizing that the Spirit is *not* always directing us in detail. The Lord does not want perfection from us, He wants FAITH and that implies an element of risk and uncertainty. God is delighted when we simply go forward, improvising by faith in the direction that aligns with His Word. Delight yourself in the Lord, and he will give you the desires of your heart. Heaven wants to empower you so that you can conceive and create inspired things! Again, it's just mind blowing that God honours the desires that are in our hearts. These desires are an early indicator of a new direction. It begins as a pull, a yearning that is in your life that will move you in the direction of what Heaven ultimately wants you to do.

Take Action

1. On each of your "Dream Pages" in your Vision Mapping Journal, describe in writing the passion you currently feel in that area. How often do you think about that dream? How important is it to you to achieve that dream?

Rate your passion level for that dream on a 0 to 10 scale. (0 = no passion, 10 = borderline obsession – you go to bed thinking about it, you wake up thinking about it, in fact, you have a hard time staying focused on other things because your mind constantly keeps drifting back to this particular dream).

2. For those "important dreams" where you sense that your level of passion is lacking, answer the following questions:

a. Do you really have a clear and precise vision of that dream?

b. Have you "converted" that dream into written goals, steps and tasks? If you have not, your hope will only be based on a wish rather than on seeing how you can accomplish your dream step by step. Without well-founded hope, there will be little sustaining passion.

c. Are you letting other people's criticisms subvert your enthusiasm and passion? If so, pay attention to the "bucket of water" module in the Personal Leverage Section.

d. Do you have a subtle or even a high "fear of failure"? If so, put that fear behind you by doing the exercises in the Personal Leverage Section.

e. Are you discouraged by your "lack of know-how" or your "lack of resources" needed to perform the tasks, take the steps, achieve the goals and accomplish the dream? If so, realize that recruiting the right partners, mentors and outside resources is critical to fuelling passion.

3. Use the Vision Mapping Journal

HONOUR

Honour is a stance and a willingness to reward someone for their difference. The 10 commandments are about honour; the first 4 deal with honouring God, the last 6 deal with honouring people. The fifth Commandment about honouring your parents guarantees a reward.

Some groups like to point to capitalism as a problem of the rich preying on the poor; however, capitalism works well as long as men have honour. It is common to see where greed has replaced honour amongst politicians, business leaders, and people in general, instead of honourable and enterprising people providing quality goods and services to create wealth for themselves. We do have politicians and scientists alike who can be bought and who become the willing paid servants of any master with an agenda. This lack of honour has infiltrated every profession, such that even "science" is no longer science, but rather a politicized practice of information distortion for financial gain. What is lacking in all of it is "honour."

A true culture of honour will disrupt the current model of authority as it is rooted in serving each other. A culture of honour celebrates and encourages everyone to see value in others; and removes the practice of false comparison or false competition in the marketplace. It is about self-control, responsibility, boundaries and confrontation.

In a business with a team, confrontation through honour will be a non-judgmental way of confronting others or team members by asking questions and helping the individual reach conclusions on what they need to change, I know that people carrying out different roles approach a problem differently and that's okay. While honour-based confrontation can be challenging as an approach to implement, it surely builds much better team connections.

A culture of connection brings out the best in others.

Jesus put it like this in Matthew 20:25-26, *'And Jesus called them to Him and said, you know that the rulers of the Gentiles lord it over them, and their great men hold them in subjection [tyrannizing over them]. Not so shall it be among you; but whoever wishes to be great among you must be your servant.'* For His leadership style, Jesus states that those with power must learn to empower those around them; this is required to build Heaven in business. Within an organization or team, the leader should honour the team and we should show honour to our leaders, as it is designed to go both directions. If it's one-way, it's unhealthy. If you want to receive and experience honour, you have to give honour and embrace humility, integrity, purity and simplicity. Honour helps you navigate obstacle after obstacle along the way, and to lead a team of loyal employees who are all committed to serving each other and their customers with honour and excellence. Honour shows businesses how to partner with its workers and consumers instead of competing against them.

Culture of Honour = Low Anxiety/Fear + High Connection + Keeping Love On = High productivity + Increase in Profit

Authors like Brené Brown, Daniel Pink, Dale Partridge, Simon Sinek and more are drawing attention to many of the toxic aspects of business culture, especially in corporations that abide by the operating principle of "profit first and people second." The culture of large corporate settings is generally one of high anxiety, high competition, and survival of the fittest. The larger the business, the more intense the corporate culture, and the less honour stays involved.

The book *Business of Honour* by Bob Hasson and Danny Silk addresses the same problem, but from a much more "up close and personal" position. Bob and Danny do their best to lay out the pillars of this culture, describe how they have worked to implement them as leaders, and share the results they have seen. Bob's hope is that readers of this book will have a heart realignment with who they are as sons and daughters of a loving Father. Common questions that I have seen around the topics of honour and business that are answered in Bob's book include:

- Why are so many business environments anxiety-driven and why do team members struggle to understand each other and function as a connected unit?
- What gives honouring people an edge in business?
- What happens when people thrive in a business culture of honour, love and safety?

Honour begins in the heart - with the core beliefs that define our identity and values. Honour is not primarily about the list of things we need to do to be more honouring, but about the heart and identity story we need to be living from to produce the fruit of honouring behaviour. This relational identity is the foundation of honour. Learning to see ourselves through the Father's eyes and receiving His love enables us to see others from the same perspective. It shifts our internal motivation from fear and self-protection to love and self-giving, which is the heartbeat of healthy relationships and teams.

Ultimately, honour is all about stewarding relationships well - and business is all about relationships. Investing in building an honouring relational culture in business is not a competitive liability, but a competitive edge. The number-one priority in a culture of honour - in business and in life - is to know the Father and show the Father. This was Jesus' number-one mission. He told His disciples, *"Anyone who has seen me has seen the Father"* (John 14:9). When I look at much of business culture, I keep coming back to this conviction that what is missing is the Father's heart.

My desire is that the culture of honour would enable people to start conversations about business with this missing piece in mind. How would we approach our productivity and performance culture differently if we were carrying more of His heart? How would it change the way members of different generations work together? How would it shape hiring and firing decisions? How would it influence the way we invest our profits? I think many things could change for the better if we especially our leaders, start thinking this way.

SPACE-TIME

Space and time are interwoven, and that's why physicists call them space-time rather than space and time. When you alter space, you invariably alter time. Space-time is a literal fabric and it is invisible; however, we could see it through our spirit eye or when God gives us spiritual eyes to see it. It is like a fabric that can be bent and worked and stretched like the surface of a trampoline. It is actually bent and warped and stretched by heavy matter such as planets.

Imagine you had a trampoline, and you took a bowling ball, and that represented a planet, and you rolled it out on the trampoline - what would the trampoline do? It would stretch and bend, right? The ball would roll down into the middle. The fabric would stretch around the bowling ball. That's what the fabric of space-time does. It is a literal unified fabric and one of its characteristics is it stretches and it bends and it warps. See the "Science Casts: Space-Time Vortex" video in the reference section or search for "A space-time vortex around Earth, presented by Science@NASA 'science.nasa.gov'".

Science

Einstein came to think of the three dimensions of space and the single dimension of time as bound together in a single fabric of space-time. It was his hope that by understanding the geometry of this four-dimensional fabric of space-time, that he could simply talk about things moving along surfaces in this space-time fabric. Space-time is a mathematical model that combines space as being three dimensions, and time as playing the role of the fourth dimensions, and they're combined with each other.

Like the surface of a trampoline, this unified fabric is warped and stretched by heavy objects like planets and stars. Einstein believed that these dimensions of space and time were linked together, and that they formed a fabric. His theories came when he was discovering things through his experiments with light.

Einstein predicted this over a hundred years ago, and it turns out to be true. On May 4th, 2011, researchers announced that NASA's Gravity Probe B spacecraft had detected the vortex, and its shape precisely matches the predictions of Einstein's theory of gravity. Time and space, according to Einstein's theories of relativity, are woven together, forming a four-dimensional fabric called space-time.

Gravity Probe B proved what Einstein believed all those years ago. Now I think it's really cool that NASA has proven that space and time are not independent of each other, and that's what the Bible says in Hebrews 1:2-3. That God created the reaches of space together with the ages of time. The Bible describes the fabric of space-time in Isaiah 40:22 - we see a description of the fabric. Imagine that! God is talking about the stuff that scientists, centuries later, would discover is true. The fabric is the divider between God, in the eternal realm, and us, here, in this temporal realm.

God has ordained sovereignly that the reaches of space, meaning every location in space, and the ages of time were created together; that they are intricately involved with each other; that they are intertwined with each other. God created all those locations in space. Every location in space, be it outer space, inner space, Paris or China, whatever space it is, he created them all. He also created the ages of time. He built them all together, and because he's the builder, he has access to all those locations and all those ages of time.

That means if Jesus Christ wants to take you someplace in the reaches of space or the ages of time, He can because He made them. Space and time are intertwined with each other, you can't separate them; when you're dealing with one, you're dealing with the other. You're going to start going back in space and time to the origin of sickness or disease or lack in your family lineage/forest, and pull out lies, wounds and trauma at the root and replacing them with the Truth. You're going to get healed, you are going to prosper and advance. It is time to advance and it's never going to come back again.

We live in three-dimensional space. Everything around us has height, depth, and width. Think of them as coordinates, coordinates, coordinates in space. If you wanted to find an aeroplane that was flying through the air, you would need to know the coordinates, right? The altitude, the longitude and the latitude. That's how you could find where that plane was at, the location of it. If you really wanted to find that plane, you couldn't just find it by knowing the altitude, the longitude, and the latitude. You'd have to know what time that plane was going to be at that altitude, longitude and latitude. If you didn't know what time it was going to be there, you would miss the plane at that location.

You're going to see as you begin to travel forward in time and back in time, you're not only just going to go to the times things happened in your family, where sickness or trauma came upon them, but you're going to go to the location where it happened, the place in space, because time and space are woven together as one.

My experience is that I began to systematically wipe out lack and iniquity in my life when the Holy Spirit would take me back to the time and place where that lack or those diseases came upon my lineage, like the village where my great-great-grandfather grew up, or the village where my grandmother grew up, even centuries back to places I never knew ever existed. And when I got to that place in time, I just knew in my spirit that somehow my ancestors were connected, my family line was connected to that place, and something traumatic had happened there. It had caused me, centuries later, to still be afflicted by that problem or iniquity. I would know that I actually went there because I would get a healing or a breakthrough when I returned. This journey to past or future occurrence did not happen on demand for me, like whenever the Holy Spirit shows me a vision of a future event while I am mending my business. It can happen anytime.

I remember as I began to experience this over again, I began to ask Jesus Christ, "Why does that happen? Why are you not only taking me back in time, but why are you are taking me to all these locations and spaces? What's the deal?" One thing He said among others is that there is a generational blessing in every bloodline that God wants to redeem and release His Father's heart. He has made tools available for us to go back in time in Christ to address sins, traumas, lack, iniquities and character bent that can hide our prosperity because the enemy can, and will, use these past or present events to build a case against us in the courts of Heaven. When a miraculous element comes into the equipping environment, Christ moves past the ordinary process of time and accelerates provision and empowerment. We are in a session where all that you have missed, you get to recapture in a brief span of time.

In terms of workplace or business growth and strategy, for space-time, Christ is the beginning and the end. He has the only name that is above all names. He knows what the systems and spaces of this world will look like in 300 or 1,000 years from now, and can take you into the future 300 years from today. However, for this to happen, it will not just be about you carving out a career or business niche, it's more like you yielding to a divine purpose that Christ shows you. It's you surrendering yourself and all your influence, access, and ability to a purpose greater than yourself. That, my friends, is a powerful proposition, and one that threatens the regions of darkness!

FIRST FRUIT

First fruits mean that at every new beginning, you honour God by giving Him the FIRST! First fruits are a key to God's blessing and it is one of the foundational principles of God's Kingdom. First fruit is in both the Old and New Testament of the Bible. Jesus Christ is the first fruit of a new creation (1 Corinthians 15:20-23) and when we seek first the kingdom of God and His righteousness, all these things shall be added to us (Matthew 6:33).

All of us go through life dealing with a lot of stuff and we all have many interests and activities. However, Jesus is not content to be one more item on your list - He wants to be 'number one' in your life and He deserves to have first place as He gave His life for you and He brings light in the darkness. Blessed is the nation whose God is the Lord - Christ is not just for a soul, He is for a city, the nations and the world.

In every new beginning you honour God first: 'When I get a new harvest, I give the first sheaf of wheat to God! 'When I get new income, I'll give a portion to God before I spend any of it.' 'In a new month, and a new year, the FIRST thing I will do is honour God!'

> *"Honour the Lord with your wealth, and with the first fruits of all your crops [income], then your barns will be abundantly filled, and your vats will overflow with new wine."* (Proverbs 3:9-10)

At a birthday party, who gets the FIRST piece of cake? The person whose birthday it is! They are the guest of honour. When I write a new book, and the first shipment arrives from the publisher, I take the first copies out the box and give to my covenant friends. I give them the first because they are people I want to honour. There are incredible promises attached to first fruits! When Israel entered the land and received its harvest, they were to put the first sheaf of wheat they harvested in a basket and take it to God's Sanctuary (Deuteronomy 26). At the sanctuary, they were to give the first fruits of their land harvest to the priest and publicly declare the goodness and faithfulness of God. And God made a promise!

*"If you will honour God by giving Him the first fruits of your harvest,
the LORD will set you high above all the nations which He has made,
for praise, fame, and honour; and you will be a people holy to the Lord."*

This shows the incredible reward for one basket of grain, something very important about first fruits. *It is important to understand the first fruit was not the LARGEST gift of the year.* When they brought in the full harvest ...1/10 of everything was God's (the TITHE). First fruits were often just one sheaf of wheat, yet it released MASSIVE BLESSING. What made it so significant? It was showing God HONOUR. It was saying, "Lord, I am giving you the FIRST! I am putting your first in my life."

What does it mean to give a first fruit offering?

1. It means to give God the FIRST, the first of your increase or profit! "Give the FIRSTFRUITS of your grain, new wine and oil ... The first wool from shearing" (Deuteronomy 18:4-5). So when you get income or new sources of increase, you give a portion of it to God first! Also: Giving to God FIRST in a new season! In a new year, new month, give something to God FIRST!
2. It should also be the BEST portion. *"Bring the BEST of the first fruits of your soil to the house of the LORD"* (Exodus 23:19).

Someone asked, 'does that apply if we're not in an agricultural economy?' What if we get a pay cheque? Remember, crops ripen all through the year: Barley in early spring, wheat in early summer, grapes in late summer, olives in the autumn, lambs were born in the spring. Each harvest was like a pay cheque, it was a reward for their labour. At each harvest, they gave the FIRST portion of their "pay cheque" to God. Hence giving first fruits doesn't mean giving your whole cheque; it means whenever you get paid you choose to honour God by giving something to Him first.

Significance of first fruits giving

- Honours God as your source – a declaration that blessings come from God.

- Sanctifies the rest of harvest – If the first fruit is holy, then the whole batch is holy (Romans 11:16).
- Releases blessing – *"Give the first portion ... so a BLESSING may rest on your household"* (Ezekiel 44:30). *"Honour the Lord ... with the first fruits of all your crops; then your barns will be filled to overflowing and your vat will brim over with new wine"* (Proverbs 3:9-10). God promises abundant blessing for those who give first fruits.

Another question about first fruits is how much do I give? "A portion" - one lamb, one sheaf, one basketful, of all that is your first and best ... give the first portion to God to honour Him for your increase!

KEY: *It's not about the amount; it's about showing honour to God by PUTTING HIM FIRST! At the start of every new beginning, ask the Lord, what can I give to honour you?*

The Bible actually describes 3 categories of giving. In Nehemiah 12:44, men were appointed to be in charge of the storerooms for:

- The contributions;
- The first fruits;
- The tithes.

All three are important. If you neglect one, you can miss the fullness of God's blessings! This may be why some people tithe, but don't see the level of blessings they expected. When it comes to biblical giving, tithing is just part of the picture.

- Tithe: Giving 10%, *an act of obedience to God.*
- First fruits: Something you give to God first, *showing Him honour.*
- Offerings: A free-will expression, *thanksgiving to God.*

Tithe + First fruits + Offerings = Blessings of God released.

One more question about first fruits: When do I give first fruits? You can give a first fruit offering any time; however, in the Bible, God provided His people with a special time. It was the monthly first fruits celebration held on the first of every month! The Jews call that monthly celebration ROSH CHODESH (Hebrew: "The head of the Month"). The Bible also calls it a "New Moon" celebration, which sounds strange. Worshipping the moon and astrology? NO!

Why does God call it a New Moon celebration?

Genesis 1 said the sun, moon and stars were given by God as <u>signs</u> to mark His appointed times. So when the ancient Jews wanted to know when a new month began, they didn't look at a calendar on the wall, they looked at the moon. God arranged for the moon to go through a complete cycle twelve times a year. This divided the year into 12 months. New month began at new moon! Every month the Jews watched for the "new moon" to appear! When they saw it. "A new month had begun"- "ROSH CHODESH". They began every new month by joining together in a joyful celebration to praise and honour God. Celebrating Rosh Chodesh, they said, "the very first thing we will do with our time this month is to joyfully celebrate to the Lord." That's called putting GOD FIRST.

The Bible says a lot about Rosh Chodesh:

- A Joyful Celebration (Hosea 2:11, Psalm 81:3-7)
- A Day of Rest - Businesses Closed (Amos 8:5)
- Special Offerings to God (Numbers 28:11-15)
- A Day of Worship (Isaiah 66:23, Numbers 10:10)
- A Day of Feasting (No Fasting) (1 Samuel 20:5)

Rosh Chodesh was a time at the start of each month to praise and honour God. It was a time to bring first fruits offerings and a time to hear what the prophets were saying about the month ahead.

Result: The Jewish people prospered. In Jesus' day, Rosh Chodesh was a very important celebration. It's a celebration that Jesus and the apostles would all have observed. Rosh Chodesh began with the sighting of the new moon - two witnesses were required. Sumptuous meals prepared in temple courts; people came to serve as witnesses. When 2 witnesses saw the new moon, the Sanhedrin declared: The new moon month has begun! They had a jubilant celebration before the Lord. Rosh Chodesh is a celebration for all time. Isaiah 66, describing the new heavens and new earth says, *"it shall come to pass, that from one new moon to another ... all flesh shall come to worship before ME, says the Lord."* Amazing - Isaiah says that in the future, all mankind (Jews and Gentile) will come together and worship JESUS at Rosh Chodesh!

Rosh Chodesh is not just for Jews! It's for all of God's people at all times! Rosh Chodesh is part of the activity of Heaven!

Rosh Chodesh was given to help us develop a mentality of first fruits! It's a way of giving God the first of our TIME each month. But it's also an occasion to bring God the first of our INCREASE! Giving God the first fruits of our money releases God's BLESSING on our finances, so giving God the first fruits of our time will attract His BLESSING on our time! *Now Rosh Chodesh is not commanded!* We are free to celebrate it or not celebrate it. But it does release God's BLESSING! This is why I celebrate first fruits every month. As we HONOUR God with the FIRST of our time, all of our time is SET APART (made special or holy). We are positioned to receive His BLESSING all through the month! And we are enabled to walk in God's BLESSING throughout the year! God WANTS your new year to be filled with His blessings!

THE SKY'S NOT THE LIMIT

Shooting for the Moon is the process of defining dreams and setting goals that are extraordinary for a person to achieve on his or her own. *It means setting goals and striving for dreams that are beyond our personal reach and even seem impossible at first glance.* "Shooting for the Moon" is so important. It is a technique that supercharges the Vision Mapping Process.

This process is powerless without utilizing the other strategies like vision mapping and effective partnership, but it is completely and fully empowered when utilized in conjunction with the other breakthrough strategies.

When you "Shoot for the Moon", if you miss, you are still a thousand times greater than the tallest mountain on earth.

Shooting for the Moon means rather than taking a job in which you live from wage to wage, where you merely show up and "do time", you're going to "swing" for a profession in which you far surpass your employer's greatest expectations. This approach covers every area of life that is important to you. For someone who wants a great marriage, instead of settling for a good marriage you shoot for a great one - a relationship where the deepest needs and desires of you and your mate are consistently fulfilled. This principle is a key component of eventually becoming a "north star" rather than a declining star.

One of many strategies that will build our wealth is "reprogramming" our mind for uncommon results. Some goal-setting plans I've seen have one severe constraint. With this particular limitation, you might multiply accomplishments and an individual's income by double or triple, however, they scarcely multiply an individual's income or accomplishments by a hundredfold or a thousandfold. You're told to set goals that were achievable and realistic. Years ago I was told that if I don't follow this 'achievable and realistic' rule and set goals that are unrealistic, I will fail to achieve them. This is perfectly sound reasoning; many have become frustrated and discouraged and have even abandoned their goal-setting programs because they set unrealistic, unachievable goals; however, the fact is if you only set achievable goals, you will never achieve uncommon success.

"If you think you can or you think you can't, you are correct" - Henry Ford

Wisdom Key:

- Dream BIGGER than you can possibly achieve;
- Set realistic, achievable goals when you want average or above average outcomes;
- "Shoot for the Moon" when you want uncommon outcomes!

Wealth creation building block:

No-one has ever achieved uncommon success without "Shooting for the Moon". Everyone who has ever achieved "impossible dreams" has done so by "Shooting for the Moon".

Summary of Steps for "Shooting for the Moon"

1. Make a choice to "Shoot for the Moon" in a specific dream, goal, project, or endeavour.

2. List the obstacles or roadblocks that may prevent you from hitting the moon on that specific dream, goal, or project that might keep you from completing specific steps or tasks that are necessary to complete to achieve a goal.

3. Identify the types of partners or outside resources you will need to recruit to overcome any of the obstacles you have listed.

4. Identify the specific individuals or resources you will try to recruit.

5. Recruit the partners or resources needed and begin to complete the steps and tasks you have listed on your Vision Map.

EFFECTIVE PARTNERSHIP

It is impossible to achieve uncommon success without effectively partnering and the era of an obsession for your own promotion is over. There is no such thing as a self-made man, every impossible dream ever achieved has come through partnering. At the core, a partnership is about agreement. Your agreements determine the quality of your life and the quality of your manifestation. Examples of agreements include:

a. Agreements you make about your identity;
b. Agreements you make about who God is;
c. Agreements with the devil at an unconscious level.

Your agreement authorizes manifestation. Agreement multiplies leverage for manifestations. When God speaks you can get a revelation, insight, word, prophecy and promise; in between this point of revelation and blessings come the presence events, or the valley, or the test. Many times when God blesses you, you may go through a situation that looks the opposite of what God has said. Your agreements can make or break you when you go through the process events.

We need to leverage other people's time, energy, skill, access and money because there is simply not enough time to do everything well and in order to build long-term wealth and success, we need effective partnership.

Partners can include counsellors, consultants, advisors, experts, authors, friends, key employees, joint venture, financiers, investors, lenders, mentors, and literal or legal partners who are recruited to fulfil tasks that are necessary to the optimal achievement of a goal, project, or dream.

An entrepreneur looking to grow their business will constantly find new individuals and organisations to help carry their vision forward. They will find a core team as soon as possible, and they partner with investors for his or her capital; they will create joint ventures with vendors and form alliances with other well-known brands to make them stand out.

Effective partnering raises the level of success exponentially, accelerates success swiftly, and reduces risk immensely.

Partnering involves some essential components:

Step 1: Think of a big objective for your own business or organization.

Step 2: Write down what's really missing from your organization.

It may as easily be a team, brand credibility, experience ... anything you lack, although it may be cash. For this example, let's say it's a team, and reverse engineer the right people in your team. Probably a lack of leads causes having less money. If you'd an extra 50 quality inbound leads a month coming through, that may solve your cash issue.

Step 3: Acknowledge that someone has an excess of what you need.

For this example, if you have a low-cost product, recognize that someone has already built a relationship with thousands of people that are your ideal target audience and someone possesses that database at the moment; likewise, someone already has products which they would happily add to your product range simply for the exposure and someone is looking for a worthy business or products to support and has a brand that is great.

Step 4: Identify the right type of partner needed for the given situation; afterwards you need to identify the right person within that partner group to form the alliance.

To do step 4, you need to:

    a. Gain a clear and precise vision;

    b. Have an accurate assessment;

    c. Establish the category of partner;

    d. Decide the role(s) the partner plays;

    e. Create a profile or description of the ideal partner;

f. Identify the right person within that type.

Step 5: Outline what's in it for them.

Before reaching out to propose a possible alliance, find out what are the issues or pain they've got which you will really help them solve. Perhaps they also want leads that are new - which means you could do a cross-promotion.

Partnerships usually are not a zero-sum game: if I send you a customer, and you send me a customer, we both end up with two customers but if I give you a pound, and you give me a pound, we both have a pound.

Step 6: Pitch them, recruiting the right person with the right kind of offer. This can be really where you get to multiply time and rapidly attain extraordinary results by working with other People of Influence – but you need an excellent pitch.

Step 7: Effectively utilizing the partner for optimal results - when any of these components are absent, partnering becomes far less effective and potentially disastrous. From history, no one has ever achieved extraordinary success without effective partnering.

It's rewarding learning the building block of pitching. How you present a deal has a huge effect on the way it's received. The wording you utilize, the materials you bring, the assembly location and the way you follow up all impact the quality of the partnerships you form.

Essential Components to Effectively Utilize Partners

1. Provide the opportunity and authority;

2. Provide the right environment;

3. Provide the right incentives;

4. Use the greatest long-term motivating strategy.

Ineffective partnering raises risk, accelerates failure and limits success. Partnering is a wealth principle for maximum achievement in minimum time.

No-one in history has ever achieved extraordinary success without effective part-nering; 100 percent of all extraordinary achievements have been accomplished through effective partnering. Effective partnering raises the level of success and wealth exponentially, accelerates success meteorically, and reduces risk enormously.

Who were Maurice Clark and Henry Flagler, Harry Sonneborn and Ubbe Iwerks? You may not recognize any of these names. You do, however, know the names of their partners who achieved their impossible dreams. In fact, none of the "famous" partners would have achieved their fame or their impossible dreams had they not teamed up with these "unknown" partners.

Without partnering, Robert Morris, George Washington and Thomas Jefferson would have never realized their impossible dream to defeat the British and liberate thirteen small colonies. There would have been no Revolutionary War, no United States of America; and one of the greatest economic and personal freedoms in the history of the world would have never been available to millions of people.

Without Maurice Clark and Henry Flagler, John D. Rockefeller would have never created Standard Oil and would have never become the richest man in the world.

Without Harry Sonneborn, Ray Kroc's dream of a McDonald's restaurant on thousands of street corners would have died an awful, profitless death after only 200 franchises had been sold.

Walt Disney arrived into Hollywood with $40 in his pocket and a suitcase of clothes, but without Ubbe Iwerks and Walt's other partner, his brother Roy Disney, there would have never been a Mickey Mouse. Without Mickey, the Disney entertainment and theme park empires would have never materialized, because Walt Disney, John D. Rockefeller and Ray Kroc discovered the unlimited power of strategic partnering, their impossible dreams became unimaginable success stories.

"Our success has really been based on partnerships from the very beginning" - Bill Gates

Wealth principle: Identify, Recruit and Effectively Utilize Partners

The Principle of Uncommon Wealth

It is impossible to achieve and maintain uncommon wealth in any arena without effectively partnering. Every extraordinary or impossible dream ever achieved and sustained has been achieved through partnering.

Some people do everything they can on their own, and they normally go with the flow - they see no need to partner. They only partner as a last resort when there is no other way to get what they want. While some work hard, they mistakenly believe that getting what they want is simply a matter of trying harder and working harder, so they pursue their dreams alone or with minimal or ineffective partnering, or occasionally partnering when they see the need to do so; but they view partnering as a weakness rather than a strength.

Uncommon achievers will set uncommon goals that they know are impossible to achieve without the recruitment of strategic partners. They view partnering as a critical part of their strategy from the very outset of their plan. Effective partnering is one of the most powerful strategies they utilize. It becomes part of their nature.

Wealth creation strategy building block:

- You cannot overcome the roadblocks of your "lack of know-how" and your "lack of resources" without the right partners.
- It is impossible to "hit the moon" without the right partners.

Benefits of Effective Partnering

1. it's the fastest and most beneficial way to overcome your lack of know-how and to remove the limits of your limited resources.

2. It raises your chances of success geometrically and level of success exponentially.

3. It accelerates your achievement of success meteorically and increases your knowledge and broadens your expertise.

4. It increases your offensive power against competitive forces and reduces your vulnerability to their attacks and also reduces your risk of failure.

5. It reduces the quantity and the degree of failures you will experience; it reduces your personal workload and It reduces your level of personal stress.

Strategies and Tips for Identifying and Recruiting the Right Partners

1. Assess your own strengths and weaknesses, then identify the talents, abilities, and strengths that you need in a partner to compensate for the areas of your weaknesses, inabilities, and lack of interest.

2. Look for a person who shares the same vision you have for your business venture or personal dream and also look at the character and integrity of your would-be partner.

3. Look for a partner who is willing to be totally committed to your vision to achieve its success.

4. Look at your would-be partner's natural drive and gifts rather than his or her resume and ask yourself whether your would-be partner a positive person or a negative person?

Reaching for Help

We all need to reach for help every now and again. Overcomers know the inevitable reward of reaching. They conquer their pride and reject the trap of isolation. Turn to God. Honour those who are qualified to help you. Your future depends on it. Reaching Is the First Sign of Humility. *Inform an Intercessor. You need a Prayer Partner.* Fighting your own battles alone is one of the biggest mistakes you could ever make. Dare to reach. Someone aches to give ... as much as you need to receive.

"Again I say unto you, That if two of you shall agree on earth as touching anything that they shall ask, it shall be done for them of My Father which is in Heaven." (Matthew 18:19)

Building Blocks of Wealth Creation include:

- Converting dreams into goals, goals into steps and steps into tasks;

- Daring to dream the impossible;

- Effectively recruiting;

- Utilizing partners to pursue those dreams.

TIMING

Time can be described as something God created to prevent event all happening at once. In terms of the human journey timeline, we could split the time outlook into time zones: Past (hindsight), Present (insight) and Future (foresight).

In all of these zones, we need to break off the shame from failure, fear, false pride and false comparisons. We don't normally conceive and give birth in the same session; the world as we know it lives in tipping session, like when you have scales at a tipping point, it does not take something weighty to tip the scales.

Timing is Everything

We need to be prepared for pivotal moments of life and recognize the times and seasons God has ordained for us.

The story is told of a man who rushed into a suburban station one morning and in breathless anticipation/with bated breath asked the ticket agent: "When does the 8:04 train leave?"

"At 8:04," was the answer.

"Well," the man replied, "it is 8:02 by my watch, 8:00 by the town clock, and 8:07 by the station clock. Which time am I to go by?"

"You can go by any clock you wish," said the agent, "but you cannot go by the 8:04 train, for it has already departed."

Time is moving forward hour by hour, minute by minute. There are multitudes who seem to think they can live by any schedule they choose and that in their own time, they can do what they need to do.

I am reminded of an event I saw in the Bible. The Bible indicates that this event happened about 1400-1500 BC; a group of Israelites decided to try and possess the land of Canaan the day after God told them the opportunity had passed.

They were routed by the Canaanites (Numbers 14:39-45). The train had already left.

The ability to understand the times gives an insight as to what to do. Very often we try to reap during planting season, plant during harvest, run when we should be resting and rest when it is time to run. This will cause us to miss the train every time.

I am also reminded of a verse I saw in the Old Testament: "Behold, I will do something new, now it will spring forth; will you not be aware of it? I will even make a roadway in the wilderness, rivers in the desert" (Isaiah 43:19). Notice the phrase 'spring forth' -these words mark a shift in time. Something new is about to spring forth. "Will you not be aware of it?" He asks. Never give up. Your shift may be closer than you think.

Also, notice the word "new"; this speaks again of a shift. In the New Testament, two Greek words are translated "new" even though they have different meanings. The word 'neos' means numerically new but not different. For instance, if you buy a brand-new Sony Z smartphone, you have a new phone, but there are hundreds more just like it all over. The other Greek word for "new" is 'kainos' - this means not only numerically new but also qualitatively new. This refers to a service or product, like the Samsung S9 smartphone manufactured today as compared to an older model like S1. The newly manufactured S9 will be numerically and qualitatively new.

Distinguishing the dynamics between these two expressions 'neos' and 'kainos' is very important in our personal and business growth. *Growth involves learning how to make distinctions that lead to productivity, multiplication, distribution and market control.*

From time to time, lobsters have to leave their shells in order to grow. They need the shell to protect them from being torn apart; yet when they grow, the old shell must be abandoned. If they did not abandon it, the old shell would soon become their prison and finally their casket. The tricky part for the lobster is the brief period of time between when the old shell is discarded and the new one is formed. During that terribly vulnerable period, the transition must be scary to the lobster. We are not so different from lobsters. To change and grow, we must sometimes shed our shells - a structure, a framework - that we've depended on.

Purpose-driven Time

The ancient Greeks had at least three words for time: chronos, kairos and pleroma.

Chronos refers to a clock time measurable resource – time that can be measured – seconds, minutes, hours, years. Kairos refers to an appointed time, an opportune moment, or a due season; where chronos is quantitative, kairos is qualitative. It measures moments, not seconds. Pleroma refers to the fullness of time. An example of pleroma is the 9 months between conception and baby delivery that a woman goes through; the last day of the 9 months represents the fullness of time, while the delivery moment is the 'kairos' time.

Kairos is the word used for time by the writer Paul in Ephesians 5:16 of the Bible:

> *"Therefore see that you walk carefully [living life with honour, purpose, and courage; shunning those who tolerate and enable evil], not as the unwise, but as wise [sensible, intelligent, discerning people], making the very most of your time [on earth, recognizing and taking advantage of each opportunity and using it with wisdom and diligence], because the days are [filled with] evil."* (Ephesians 5:15-16 Amplified Bible)

Mindset Shift

What will the days to come bring to your life? We are not supposed to wait passively and see what the day brings to our life, we need to number, prepare and appoint our days before they happen. Before our days happened God prepared them, He purposed and appointed them - we must do likewise through prayer. Prayer is not only for what is but also what is not yet. You appoint your days in God to bring what is good, you consecrate them for the purposes of God, and then you use your days to accomplish these purposes. Don't let your day determine your life, let your life determine your days. Don't just let your days go by, prepare your days that they may become vessels of blessings and life. Before the first days happened, God prepared them. Teach us to number our days - numbering our days requires us to make a mental shift. Not every second holds the same worth. Some see their time like grains of sand slipping through an hourglass or as seconds ticking by. We need to realize that not every second holds the same worth - some moments are more valuable than other moments. We have to take advantage of our kairos and pleroma opportunities.

This requires us to make a mental shift. We must change our view of what effectiveness really is - effectiveness is not necessarily ramming as much as we can into 24 hours. It's not us ploughing the field with as much vigour as we can muster. The effective steward is a focused watchman whose senses are attuned to the slightest hint of an opportunity. He's a hawk on the lookout. The effective steward not only recognizes these kairos opportunities but has the courage to leap upon them with all his might. And the effective steward has organized his schedule in such a way that leaves him open to seizing these opportunities.

Wisdom keys

- Don't let your diligence towards chronos choke out your attention to kairos.
- Find your Shabbat, a day of rest in the week (especially when you get messed up), in order to break the cycle of warfare you have been pressing through, and get renewed at the feet of the Holy Spirit.

Most adults push through their entire life without clearly defining their desired destinations and following a map to reach them. They simply point themselves in a particular direction and start driving. They let circumstances and other people dictate where they go and when to change their direction; however, when they have a vacation they take the time and effort to determine their destinations, routes and plan, but miss the opportunities to fulfil their dreams for the other 42-51 weeks of the year, year in and year out.

Defining dreams and giving them structure and purpose is a skill. If you are part of the 96% who have not clearly defined your dreams and goals and have not created a map and a plan to achieve them, you will only achieve a tiny fraction of what is possible for you to achieve. Regardless of how long you've been one of the 96%, you can leave that group forever, beginning right now. You can become part of the 4% who achieve much more of their goals and dreams. You can stop being one of the 96% who goes through life with no purpose or direction over their short-term or long-term destinations. Keys to use include the skill of declaring your dreams and learning to use the skill of vision mapping.

Create a list of the most important areas of your life

The first step in this process of defining and mapping your dreams is to create a list of the most important areas of your life and to then prioritize that list. It is a simple thing to write down the important areas of your life. What interests you? What matters most? You may have as few as three or four important areas in your life or as many as ten, fifteen or more. For the important things on your prioritized list, macro and micro schedules.

Taking Control of Your Time

Taking control of your time is a relatively simple thing to do, and yet fewer than five percent of the population do it. Why? First, they don't recognize the importance of it and second, they don't know how to do it. Hopefully, you recognize that taking control of your time is critical to achieving your dreams. Now we will focus on the "How To's". It is not complicated, but it requires learning a few techniques and using a daily planner the right way.

If you can't control your time, you won't achieve extraordinary success or wealth.

Three Keys to Taking and Maintaining Control of Your Life

1. Replacing an illusion with reality

2. Recognize your dwindling time bank account

3. Priority planning – the key to taking control. a) Create a plan for the day, month and year. b) Execute the plan according to your priorities

Create an effective priority plan for each day, week, month and year.

Starting with your day, spend a few minutes each night planning and prioritizing your daily tasks and activities for the next day. This simple system can be written on a piece of paper, a journal or a calendar.

1. Make a list of all the tasks that you would like to accomplish that day without regard to their priority.

2. After you have created the task list, place an "A" beside the most important tasks on that list. Then place a "B" beside the tasks that are of secondary importance. Finally, place a "C" by the tasks that are the least important.

3. Now, starting with your "A" tasks, place a 1 next to your highest priority "A" task, a 2 beside the next highest priority "A" task, and so on. After you have numbered all the "A's", number all the "B's" starting with a 1 for your highest priority "B" task. After you have prioritized your "B" tasks, prioritize your "C" tasks in the same manner.

4. Execute your day according to your priorities, rather than according to your urgencies.

The best plans in the world are worthless if they are not effectively executed.

Create a macro schedule for your chronos time for completing the strategic elements of your vision.

This will involve monthly, quarterly and yearly milestones within your chart pipeline:

1. Build your schedule from the bottom up. Assign target dates for tasks first, then for the completion of each step, then for the completion of each goal and then for the final achievement of the dream. In other words, you start at the bottom and work up. This is assuming you have done the vision map.

2. Be flexible and realistic when assigning target dates, don't assign target dates that are so hard to hit, that you are likely to miss them. If

you see that you're falling hopelessly behind on a target date, either recruit help from others or move your target dates back.

Create a micro-schedule for your chronos time for completing the tactical elements of your vision.

This will involve daily/weekly activities:

1. Decide and make a list of daily and weekly habits you need to form and adapt; brainstorm on new habits as not all habits are born equal. Create a 63-day cycle for each habit formation. Make a daily to-do list each morning and limit your non-crucial phone calls to 5 minutes. Keep an idea notebook with you at all times and record your thoughts and ideas. *The right habits will decide your future.*
2. Take your day and divide it up into a 24-hour timetable and block out time for various important activities.

One of the secrets to success in your area of interest is in your daily routines, create new habits to go to the next level. Block out time to build a legacy, for meditation, worship, rest/sleep, holidays. It is about layering the blocking block /brick one at a time.

Do we really have to go into this much detail in writing?

The answer is "absolutely yes!" and "absolutely no!" If you have an important dream that you really want to achieve in a reasonable amount of time, the answer is yes. If you're pursuing a relatively unimportant or easily achieved goal, the answer is no.

FOCUS, STEWARDSHIP AND SEEDING

MORE FOCUS AND LESS STRESS

Reduce stress, increase patience and loving-kindness. You need to clear the machine. As a child, I remember my dad had an old calculator where you had to tab the clear button to clear out all the former calculations so the memory was clear and you could start over. The brain works the same way. If your mind is cluttered with many different thoughts, ideas and tasks, you will not be performing at optimum levels. You will not have focus, patience, or loving-kindness. We need to clear the machine. How do we clear the machine? It relates to our brain:

1. Clear the clutter. Clutter in your external environment causes clutter in your brain. It has been shown that a clear work desk or workspace leaves your mind, less distracted and better focused.

2. Reduce the complexity in your life: get rid of or outsource unnecessary or lower priority tasks, obligations, activities and relationships. This does not mean you don't love people - the saying "you can do anything you want but you can't do everything you want" is true for a reason. We tend to believe we can have it all and do everything. You need to choose what is most important to you and focus mainly on the very big priorities that are most important in your life so you can reduce the complexity in other areas of life.

3. Expand the silence: In this generation, we live in a sea of noise. Podcast, radio, TV, Internet, News Channels, hundreds of books on the Kindle, thousands of marketing messages a day being thrown at us through various form of media - we can't ride in the car without listening to something. We are awash in a sea of noise. When was the last time you were in silence? If you commute in a car try driving with no music, no podcast, no spoken words playing, try taking a walk in the woods, expand the silence if you need to clear your machine. When you expand the silence you will discover a space, a

73

peace and a clearing of your mind that will make you more productive, more patient and more kind in the process. I pray God blesses you with a clear, focused mind.

Wisdom Key:

Stay Focused. The secret of every success is total focus. Be ruthless with distractions. You cannot meditate on your past and your future at the same time. So, focus on your desired future.

STEWARDSHIP

We all have stewardship over time, relationships, space and wealth. Stewardship requires diligence. The story of Mayer Amschel Rothschild shows he understood the law of stewardship. Rothschild was a banker who had five sons, who grew up around Frankfurt, Germany. He would only loan money to his descendants, and after his sons moved out to five different capital cities in Europe. They created reports on the things they had learnt about capital and doing business and yearly they went back to Frankfurt to show and tell what they had learnt so the rest of the family could keep up with what was happening in the world. The story of Cornelius Vanderbilt and stewardship was not the same as Amschel Rothschild, in terms of empowering his family and people around him to build and maintain wealth.

By 1877 Cornelius Vanderbilt had a massive fortune of 105 million dollars. In order to understand what kind of fortune Cornelius held, one has to comprehend that in that time in history prices of goods and service were far lower than they are today and the whole American economy was worth some $9 billion dollars. By 1975 there was only one known millionaire among the 120 descendants of Cornelius, as in the middle of 20th century the Vanderbilts suffered major losses - their fortune and the business empire that took centuries to build was torn down in decades.

The Law of Use

Once we understand how the enemy stole from us, we have a right to get back, double, quadruple or 7 times back. The laws of use and recovery work together.

The law of use is an active law; it is also a principle that operates around and within us. Like the law of gravity, if I jump I am not going up. The law of use is "*Anything not used is lost*" - having is using. It is active possession as anything not used accumulates loss. We should only keep things that will help us move forward. If you have something you have to use it. Most people get hung up here as judgement happens when we misuse or don't use what we have. Think of one possession or talent you have. How are you using that talent?

We also need to use the issues of the past against the enemy of the future in a reconciled manner. In every new season, there is a war with the old paradigm. Moving from the old wine to present truth requires war. The old wine empowers the law of religion to set itself against your talent and wealth. The law of religion is active against the law of use. What happens with religion is that you get to a place and you think you have got it and you settle down. The moment you settle down and think you know and get it, you have come into agreement with religious spirits. No shift will happen.

There are moments to capture the revelation that will shift your future and then you will advance.

Heaven is always ready to give, to pour down revelation so we can uncover what is not clear in our life and advance. Revelation is the opposite of the occult. The occult will hide things, revelation uncovers. If you are afraid of the dark world everything will stay hidden. We are to use what we have to bring light into the darkness.

The law of use is:

a. A physical law: Unemployed strength diminishes (Luke 19:11);
b. A mental law: The successful teacher is an eager learner. The minute a teacher stops to learn he or she really has nothing to teach except last sessions manna; there is no more movement in him or her. Inactivity in the thinking process means the person is not willing to go to the next level to learn - it is the retirement mentality. It is better to retire from one and pick up another.
c. A moral law: Character is not inheritance. You don't inherit character;

you have to operate in use to develop character as evil never sleeps. Evil uses every moment, every resource, does not take vacations and is working against us all the time. The enemy can't touch character and integrity.

d. A commercial law; Keeping and multiplying is harder than getting. We have to learn how to keep and multiply everything we have (Matthew 25).

"Then another came and said, 'Lord, here is your mina, which I have kept laid up in a handkerchief [for safekeeping]. I was [always] afraid of you because you are a stern man; you pick up what you did not lay down and you reap what you did not sow; He said to the servant, 'I will judge and condemn you by your own words, you worthless servant! Did you [really] know that I was a stern man, picking up what I did not lay down and reaping what I did not sow? Then why did you not [at the very least] put my money in a bank? Then on my return, I would have collected it with interest.' Then he said to the bystanders, 'Take the mina away from him and give it to the one who has the ten minas.' And they said to him, 'Lord, he has ten minas already!' [Jesus explained,] 'I tell you that to everyone who has [because he valued his gifts from God and has used them wisely], more will be given; but from the one who does not have [because he disregarded his gifts from God], even what he has will be taken away.' (Luke 19:20-26)

SEEDING

"Make no mistake about it, God will never be mocked! For what you plant will always be the very thing you harvest." (Galatians 6:7 TPT Bible)

A seed means beginning. Seeding is a trade-out where a seed is planted for a harvest. Every farmer trades his seed for a harvest. A farmer that wants a corn harvest will sow corn seeds. A young husband plants a seed in the womb of his wife and they get a child. Everything God has given you is a seed for something else, the greatest of words begins with the smallest of letters; in the same way.

the greatest of God's work begins with the smallest of strokes. A question is the seed for a new season.

Everything on the earth is a seed. Listening is my seed for knowledge and knowledge is my seed for skill and change. My words are the seed for feelings, deliverance, breakthrough and abundance. When you sow love, you will reap love. My words create light or darkness. Forgiveness is my seed for mercy, repentance my seed for restoration. Honour is the seed for strong relationships, divine rewards, human's rewards and longevity. God had a Son, He wanted a family, and He planted His Son to create a family. Respect the law of sowing and reaping. This scriptural law of sowing and reaping is universal. Fools deny it, rebels defy it and the wise live by it. Inventory your seeds of time, mercy, honour and finances. Sow into quality soil lavishly and harvest is inevitable. I have broken the back of poverty with seeds. There is already an oak tree in the acorn, you have to show up with faithfulness.

When an investor is involved in a business' liquidity and solvency, an existing business will need seed capital for various parts of its division (building block), though seed capital for a start-up business normally involves a higher risk than standard venture capital funding as the investor does not see any existing projects to evaluate for funding. Hence, the investments made are usually lower as against normal venture capital investment for similar levels of stake in the company.

Seed funding can be raised through various channels - online platforms are available for equity and crowd-funding[1]. Investors make their decision whether to fund a project based on the perceived strength of the concept and the capabilities, skills and history of the founders.

---

1. https://en.wikipedia.org/wiki/Equity_crowdfunding

HEAVEN IN BUSINESS AND FAITH

Within a footstool lies a cosmic revelation - abundantly cosmic to be spoken of by God. 'Heaven is My throne,' He said, 'and the earth is My footstool' (Isaiah 66:1). What do you think it means?" Heaven is His throne, His dwelling place, where He rests His weight and the centre of His presence. The word for *weight* in Hebrew is '*kavode*.' *Kavode* also means glory. Heaven is the place where God's weight and glory rest. The earth is not His throne hence the earth can't bear the weight of His glory, the earth is His footstool, He rests His feet on it. It bears the imprint of His feet but never His full weight. We live in a footstool world - the earth is a footstool. It is not the place on which you can rest all your weight or your well-being. Earthly possessions, issues and problems are only footstool possessions, problems and issues. Earthly glory is only a footstool glory. You don't sit on a footstool; you sit in Heaven (Ephesians 2:6). You only place your foot on a footstool world on top of all its problems, issues and fading glories. You place your weight in Heaven and live lightly on the earth, that's the way to live.

Heaven in Business

Think Like Heaven

The culture of Heaven sustains the miraculous. The more we think and look like Heaven the more Heaven wants to be with us. Heaven is the source of every perfect thing; we need to grow in awareness and discernment and perspective of what is perfect (God), good (acceptable), permissible and evil, understanding how to respond in faith (the faith of God) and knowing that the answers to problems can come in seed form, and then stay on course to see the breakthrough.

The Source and Discernment

God is communicating to us non-stop, with unrelenting enthusiasm. *It is common to see the right revelation from God and wrong interpretation from us.* Again, the reason we do not perceive the full expression of His Person is that He reveals Himself on wavelengths we have not learned to recognize and receive.

We need to abandon the old question, 'Why isn't God talking to me? Sometimes, God sounds like you because he flows through you. Most times when God speaks, it is not the voice that is different, it is the source. We need to learn to make the distinction. The truth is for those that have trained themselves, through exercise and intimacy, deep will call unto the deep. Sometimes our perception is blurred because of the filters (human spirits that are defiled, soul wounds, offenses, strongholds, bitter roots and images in the soul). To create and sustain the atmosphere of miraculous where the glory of God takes preeminence we need to be hearing, seeing and sensing Heaven's blueprint per scenario and aligning with it. The glory of God lifts the earthly limits off of our lives and teaches us to live from a higher, heavenly place.

"I've concluded that such a proficient communicator as God is 'speaking' in a million ways, His voice filling every atom in the universe. My concern is not that God remains silent, but rather that He's talking to us on so many levels that we do not know how to interpret the spiritual bandwidths through which He communicates"
- Larry Randolph

Everything we need for life has already been accomplished by Christ on the cross. We don't need to live like drifters in any area of our lives. We can live in authority as sons and daughters and receive every blessing and walk in dominion in Christ in the heavenly places. If you are like me, Heaven is not just a place you go to when you die, it is a coexisting reality.

> *"Every good gift and every perfect gift is from above, and cometh down from the Father of lights, with whom is no variableness, neither shadow of turning."* (James 1:17)

The godly supernatural on earth is Heaven invading earth for our good. Light is huge in Heaven - food, bodies and a lot more are made out of light in Heaven. Heaven is full of fun. There is so much in the realm of inventions and discoveries that the earth is yet to receive from Heaven; this includes cures for all deadly diseases. I firmly believe that in days ahead the earth will learn from Heaven how to use light to make things we never thought possible. The earth gets it sustenance from Heaven. Knowing what heaven is thinking and aligning with it will open the door to abundance. Heaven is able to replicate itself on earth through men that lead from the future. Awareness is required in understanding that Heaven is speaking to earth. God wants to interact with us from Heaven to earth.

Awareness and Revelation

Studies have shown a percentage of our awakening hours are spent daydreaming. In the middle of the daydream are destiny dreams, when we become aware that though we were "daydreaming", but that Heaven is also speaking, then we can access heaven's thoughts. In practical terms, it is also important to be aware that whenever we properly capture a thought, we play out the thought to the end in our mind. For example, instead of thinking I hope this flight does not crash, we should think of the best-expected ending, and not give room to worry - worry is using our imagination in a negative way. Revelation is the highest type of knowledge; it is the voice and thought of God in our spirit.

> *"For My thoughts are not your thoughts, neither are your ways My ways, saith the Lord. For as the Heavens are higher than the earth, so are My ways higher than your ways, and My thoughts than your thoughts."* (Isaiah 55:8-9)

Some people wonder why God doesn't always speak in more open terms - audibly, with visible signs. The Bible indicates that God receives more glory when He conceals, rather than making things obvious. It is more glorious for Him to hide things for us, and have us seek. In the introduction to the parable of the seed and the sower we find that Jesus did not merely use parables as illustrations, but at times to conceal truth so that only the hungry would understand truth (Matthew 13:11,18-23).

It is the mercy of God to withhold revelation for those who have no hunger for truth because the chances are they won't obey it when they hear it, as revelation always brings responsibility. By keeping revelation from those without hunger, God protects them from certain failure to carry the responsibility it would lay on them. Yet, He doesn't conceal from us; He conceals for us! *"It's the glory of kings to search out a matter"* (Proverbs 25:2). We are kings and priests to our God (Revelation 1:6). Our royal identity shines brighter when we pursue hidden things with the confidence that we have legal access to such things. Mysteries are our inheritance in Christ. Our role in ruling and reigning with Christ comes to the forefront when we seek Him for answers to the dilemmas of the world. It is imperative to note that ruling from God's perspective means "to be the servant of all." Jesus answered them, *"To you it has been granted to know the mysteries of the kingdom of heaven, but to them it has not be granted"* (Matthew 13:11 NASB). The realm of God's mysteries (hidden things) is placed in waiting for the believer to discover.

Responding to Heaven

It is important we all get thoughts from God. Become aware of heavenly thoughts that are already coming to you, so you can capture them and will be able to act on them. When we can see God clearly then we can see the circumstance around us differently. When we entertain a thought long enough it becomes an action - actions eventually became habits. The habit will sow into our character and our character will sow into our destiny. When we hear from God everything can change in our life. God's thoughts carry His power to cause us to be transformed and to cut a path for us to advance. Everyone is created to hear God's voice and to speak what God speaks. Some people train themselves more on their hobbies like their favourite sport and don't give much time to training their facilities on hearing God, which is rather unfortunate. *"But solid food is for the [spiritually] mature, whose senses are trained by practice to distinguish between what is morally good and what is evil"* (Hebrew 5:14).

We do not always know the full picture by ourselves; we hear in part and prophesy in part. As your sphere of influence expands, so does the weight of what heaven speaks to you. We need to fully operate in the spirit of the influence we have before moving up. Now is the time like never before to know God's voice - the world needs people who know how to discern the voice of God clearly. By hearing the voice of God we can cut years in the process of maturing and getting into our destiny. We can advance faster in life when we learn to hear God clearly. God will reveal to you what you need to know, right now, to advance to the next level! Heaven wants to equip you to walk in your identity and destiny, to activate you to shift atmospheres over your life, your relationships and dreams. Accept that something will be unexplainable. Although you can select some of your miracles, only God can choose the method or means by which He sends it to you. In one instance Jesus used clay and spittle in the healing of the blind man. His methods can be puzzling to the natural mind and those who argue over the methods of God rarely receive the miracles of God.

Things That Can Derail Our Response to Heaven

A lack of understanding of the timing of what you are hearing from God, not having a foundation that helps you test what you are hearing, seeing and sensing, over-interpreting what Heaven is saying, over-responding or doing nothing at all.

Faith

Faith is the substance maker of things hoped for. Faith is the physical manifestation of an idea brought into being through the power of creative utterance. Faith is picturing it done. I am reminded of the story of Abraham (2166-1991 BC). Abraham went forth not knowing where he was going; he was a man of faith, being led by God into a solution that he was to manifest. Faith in action is a risk - this risk was demonstrated by Abraham. The history of the Jewish people begins when God promised a nomad leader called Abram that he would be the father of a great people if he did as God told him.

Faith is not mental - a spiritual miracle demands a spiritual act of faith; a financial miracle demands a financial act of faith. Pursuit is the proof of desire. You only reach for something that matters. God does not respond to need nor to tears, He does respond to faith. The proof of faith is the willingness to reach.

> *"Ask, and the gift is yours. Seek, and you'll discover. Knock, and the door will be opened for you. For every persistent one will get what he asks for."* (Matthew 7:7,8a the Passion Translation Bible)

Ask reveals that you are a single question away from the solution. Seek indicates that you must leave where you are, the place of comfort, to experience the answer. Knocking on the door reveals that someone is trying to stop you from discovery. The most important thing on earth is the question you are willing to ask. Faith is voice-activated. Master your miracle-talk ... every hour all day long.

God always keeps His appointments. Expect something incredible to happen today - it is time.

Create a Miracle Climate

Sound is essential in creating change. When you control the sounds around you, you control the flow of your feelings and awareness. Doubt tolerated is faith contaminated. Meditation, praise and worship can unlock your faith for miracles. Anointed music, unity and honour will expedite a miracle climate.

ACCOUNTABILITY, CONTROL AND PERSISTENCE

ACCOUNTABILITY AND CONTROL

Have you felt like what you do with the hours of your days are determined or dictated by circumstances or the needs, desires and demands of other people? For some people, this happens nearly every weekday of the month, every month of the year, and for most of their life. What they accomplish in a day, a year, and in their lifetime is not determined by their values and priorities, but rather by the demands, values and priorities of others. The tragedy is these people do not wake up to the fact that their life has been controlled by others until it is too late to achieve their most important dreams; dreams that reflect their personal values and priorities. At the end of their lives, they think, "What happened? Where did the time go? What happened to my values, my commitments, my priorities? What happened with my husband or wife? What happened with my children? What happened to my career? What happened to all the things I wanted to do, but never did? How can this be?"

As tragic as this is, it MAY happen to you, unless you stand up and take control of your life right now! But to gain control of your life, you must first take control of your time. And even though that is a very simple thing to do, it won't happen automatically. You have to take three simple steps. First, you must realize how time "gets away" from you. Second, you must learn how to capture or take control of it. Finally, you must act on that knowledge and actually begin taking control of it.

How Does Time "Get Away" From Us?

1. We Unintentionally Lose Minutes and Intentionally Throw Away Hours

Time gets away from us in both small and large increments. We accidentally let go of time in seconds or minutes and purposely throw away time in larger increments, usually in half-hours, hours or longer. We let go of time by letting our mind drift or wander out of the present, either sliding back into the past or jumping ahead into the future and we miss the incredible power of the present.

How often during the day are you doing something or listening to someone, when your mind begins to think of an upcoming weekend, or an event that took place earlier in the day or week? Each time that happens, you miss key opportunities in the present. You miss opportunities to think of something significant about a current project, opportunities to pick up a key statement of the person you're listening to. Time is our most limited resource. Often times we sacrifice the best use of our time by choosing to allocate a block of time to a merely convenient or good use of that time. Too many times, a "good" use of our limited resources is often the worst enemy and "robber" of the best use of those resources.

2. We Don't Plan and Prioritize Our Day Before It Starts

The second way time gets away from us is that we don't plan and prioritize our day before that day starts. Most people enter each day haphazardly, figuring they will simply do whatever it takes to handle each event that comes their way, as it comes. While this approach is very easy because it follows our natural inclinations, it is also very inefficient and particularly less productive. Think for a minute about the last time you went on a vacation. When did you decide where you were going to go, how you were going to get there, what you were going to do once you were there and your return home? I'm sure all of those important decisions were made before you climbed into your car or went to the airport. You had your schedule all mapped out. You had thought of most or all of the things you wanted to do and people or places you wanted to visit. It would be ridiculous to show up at the airport the day you are leaving for your vacation without any of that figured out.

And yet, as ridiculous as that scenario is, it is the way most adults start their day and face each event of every day. No wonder they feel "out of control". What makes this even more ridiculous is the fact that none of these people approaches their vacation in that manner. All of the major decisions are determined and planned out in advance. If you want to gain control of your life, you must begin to effectively plan and prioritize your days before you start each day.

3. Our Time is "Snatched" by Time Robbers

"Time Robbers" are those activities, circumstances and events that break into our day and steal our time or attention away from doing that which is most important. The Vision Mapping process will help to identify your "Time Robbers" and create a plan to protect you from their stealing your time.

4. We Allow "Urgencies" to Take Precedence over Priorities

Another way time gets away is that we let "Urgencies" take time away from our priorities. "Urgencies" are those events that demand our immediate attention and action. They may be totally insignificant, but they still jump out at us and say, "I want your attention and I want it NOW!" Mobile calls are perhaps the best example of this. We can be in the middle of a critical conversation with our spouse, our children or a business client, and no matter how important that conversation may be, if the phone rings and we stop everything and pick it up, this would be literally letting the tail wag the dog. If we are to take control of our time, we must begin to recognize that many "Urgencies" are like people who cut in front of us in a line. They may think their needs are more important, we can begin to tell our "Urgencies" to take a number and go to the back of the line.

5. We Procrastinate and Put the Most Important Things Off Until Later

Additionally, we let time get away from through procrastination. Just as we let "Urgencies" cut in front of our line, we put our priorities in the back of the line. So "Urgencies" are always dealt with NOW, and priorities are nearly always left until later. And unfortunately, for most of our priorities, later never comes. According to Hyrum W. Smith we usually postpone an important activity for one or more of the following six reasons:

1. We sense no urgency in the activity, even if it's one of our highest priorities;

2. The activity may not be fun or pleasant;

3. The activity is outside of our comfort zone;

4. We fear failure in the performance of the activity;

5. We don't perceive the activity's real value;

6. We lack the knowledge that is needed to do that activity now.

One tip that Hyrum gives for overcoming our tendency to procrastinate is to schedule those things you are likely to put off, first. By scheduling them first, we not only get them out the way, but we are then free to do other things which are more fulfilling and fun, without the weight of the guilt or fear that comes with procrastination.

To become an uncommon achiever...

1. You need to set extraordinary to impossible goals in the areas of your greatest interest.
2. Control nearly every aspect of your time, the direction of your paths, and the speed at which you move down those paths.

Wisdom Keys:

- Unless we choose to take control of our lives, our lives will be controlled by the desires, demands, values and priorities of others.
- We accidentally lose minutes by not focusing on the present, and we purposely throw away hours, accepting good uses of our "elective" times in place of "best" uses of those times.

Personal Accountability and Development

Taking a personal inventory of your time is key to maintaining control of your time. Follow a process for time inventory to do your inventory and compare the weekly logs to see patterns. The intentions for personal development include: 1. You grow 2. You are empowered to help other people grow.

PERSISTENCE

"For every persistent one will get what he asks for. Every persistent seeker will discover what he longs for. And everyone who knocks persistently will one day find an open door." (Matthew 7:8 TPT Bible)

Persistence is "the act of persisting". While perseverance is a steady persistence in a course of action, a purpose, a state, etc., especially in spite of difficulties, obstacles, or discouragement. By perseverance, the snail reached the Ark. This is an inner fire that does not quench. A persistent person is stubborn to his cause. He is the one with a goal as the "fuel" that refuels his consuming ambers. When you have an opportunity to serve you don't complain about the work involved. When you knock at the door of opportunity do not be surprised it is work who answers the door.

Adopt the Challenge Mindset

We all need to become master warriors, as we will never out-grow warfare. We need to sit at the feet of the Holy Spirit and receive his mentorship to be able to endure and be persistent. We need to wait on the Holy Spirit daily, to learn his battle techniques as we must simply learn to fight. Your endurance makes your enemy tired; the invisible quality of champions is endurance. They refuse to run from a fight and they know that overcoming involves more than one battle. Never consider quitting. Rest ... then get up again. Hell fears a fighter.

One of the secrets to winning most of the time is persistence.

What is your new habit or routine to stoke that dream or desire?

• What is the habit?

• What is the routine?

• How are you stoking your dream or desire?

If you can't show evidence of how you are daily stoking the dream I don't believe you are serious about the dream. Pause right now and think about it. What is the new habit or routine that you will use to revisit your dreams daily? Now stick to it - so many people have intermittent desire and discipline.

Take your big three goals and with each, on a scale of one to ten, ask yourself what level of discipline have you been bringing to make them happen? Think daily about the priorities, people and projects you are working through in alignment with your overall vision.

'Discipline is the bridge between goals and accomplishment' - Jim Rohn

Don't wait for happiness, generate it by revisiting your dreams. What you focus on grows - in so many ways progress towards our goals makes us feel better and makes us treat other people better.

However, there is a realm around us that is filled with accusations, depression, worry and all the stuff that is associated with darkness and lawlessness that we hate to deal with. You can't avoid it, but you can go above it. When you mount up with wings of an eagle you go above it. All of a sudden the voices and clamour go away. The wind of the Holy Spirit will need to fill your wings daily and take you above this realm of darkness and lawlessness.

> *"He giveth power to the weak; and to them that have no might he increases strength, Even the youths shall faint and be weary, And the young men shall utterly fall, But those who wait on the Lord shall renew their strength; They shall mount up with wings likes eagles, They shall run and not be weary, They shall walk and not faint."* (Isaiah 40:29-31)

When you feel faint, expect supernatural intervention; expect the supernatural in your life. Angels are assigned to you, ask your angels for help. When you go to sleep ask your angels to go and search out the land and come back with the blueprint on how to advance. Never underestimate the attentiveness of your father (God) toward you.

Most employees and sole traders tend to be preoccupied with security; this form of security is something motivated by fear. Most business owners and investors have a challenge mindset and have learnt how to embrace risk, as an investor sometimes you win, sometimes you learn how not to fail. The more failure you experience and overcome, the quicker you learn how to succeed.

If you want more discipline ...

1. Understand that every day matters: I believe every day matters because I have lost a lot of days, people I care about and opportunities. Make each day your masterpiece. If you remember how important the day is, you don't have to

squander it anymore. 'Every day matters' is a growth mindset. When every day matters, you make very different choices. When you know that at the end of your life you will ask yourself questions about how you have spent your life, you will see each day differently. Make value-based decisions for each other.

2. Raise your ambitions: The reason why a lot of people are not disciplined is because they are not trying anything significant that will inspire the discipline. You have to have a big dream to pull yourself out of self-pity, slumber and the list goes on. You can't just rely on your mood to make you disciplined because that will be a dangerous place to be. Have something that pulls you which will give you the inspiration. People on the path of purpose don't have time for dreamers or fantasists, because for them the bigger mission washes away all the silliness. Raise your ambition to stay disciplined. People get caught in negativity when they don't have any important thing to fight for - the big goal makes them forgo smaller issues.

Once you have a big ambition and it is real for you, you start adopting the challenge mindset. *The mindset says, 'I am willing to challenge myself here because I know I will grow and contribute.'*

In the study of verified high performers that measured the mind, behaviour and routine, one thing they all have in common is 'love of challenge'; when challenge and adversity came up they liked it. Where there is struggle, there is honour. As an overall global culture, we have lost the challenge mindset, and we have adapted the complaint and comfort mindset. In the old Roman Empire people loved challenges; in today's western world the tendency is for people to freak out or complain about any inconvenience or small thing.

"The journey to greatness often begins the moment that Challenge and Contribution override comfort" - Brendon Burchard

For some, when they initiate a project or a relationship and they don't see near instant success, they give up and move on to the next project or relationship. The same is true when it comes to the pursuit of dreams. When a dream isn't quickly fulfilled, it is quickly diminished, postponed or abandoned altogether.

This factor in itself is one of the biggest reasons why most people never achieve their dreams.

It is good to persevere when the goal in mind is a goal that would bring a needful and useful change. Take a look at the making of air transport system: The Wright Brothers, for example, were seen by their peers as "insane." Some of those who "loved" them tried to confine them; out of their ignorance in the quarters reserved for the mentally deranged members of society. The ignorant masses could neither accept nor understand the sophisticated wave of revolution which was sweeping through the minds of the two brothers. Though those "friends" of the Wright Brothers did what they did "out of love", they did what they did, not knowing that they were dragging human progress a thousand years behind timeline! One would wonder how many human breakthroughs have been adeptly hindered by well-meaning friends and relatives due to ignorance. Thanks to the Wright Brothers' stubborn rebellion, the two men closed their ears to the "good and wise" advice from uninformed psychoanalysts who knew better about "human behaviour" but knew nothing about inventive persistence.

You Don't Need Persistence "Down Hill", But You Cannot Go "Up Hill" Without It

Dreams are always perched on the rocks at the top of the highest mountains. They simply cannot be reached without persistence. The pathways are often steep and treacherous, filled with boulders and other obstacles. If you hope to achieve any of your dreams, you must learn how to ignite this powerful engine, and keep it burning until you successfully reach each dream. Dreams are never found lying on the floor of a valley. They are never reached by walking downhill, by coasting on cruise control, or by following the path of least resistance.

Wisdom Keys:

1. Worthwhile dreams are always found on the tops of rugged mountains, never on the valley floors.
2. Worthwhile dreams can never be achieved without encountering Strikeouts, Criticisms, Obstacles and Roadblocks.

3. Motivation gets you in the game - habits keep you there.

What Persistence is NOT:

When failure is contemplated, persistence is not simply a matter of staying the course no matter what. When failure is experienced, persistence is not simply refusing to give up and then trying the same thing over and over again, but with more effort, intensity, or frequency.

What True Persistence *IS:*

When failure is contemplated, true persistence makes the necessary mid-course corrections to reduce risk and increase the possibility of success. When failure is experienced, true persistence analyses various elements or factors that may have caused or contributed to that failure and then designs and tries creative alternatives that might result in significant improvement and ultimate success. This means when you hit a brick wall, get up, dust off and realise you are going to have to develop a creative alternative to get over, under, or around the wall. If that fails, then blow it up!

How people deal with problems, setbacks, and potential or realized failures ascertain if they become an uncommon achiever; some people quickly change course, retreat or give up and move on to the next project. While for some, if they see a hope of overcoming the problem or reversing a failure, they try harder, making additional attempts to succeed, before giving up. Uncommon achievers will do their utmost to overcome problems and setbacks and power their way through failure, to succeed in one way or another. They hardly surrender to failure even when they know that succeeding is still a long way coming. An uncommon achiever like President Donald J. Trump, one of my heroes when it comes to persistence and comeback, will approach each important project expecting problems, setbacks, and potential failure to block the path to success. They utilize their partnering skills to draw on the creative input and resources of others to creatively persist through each problem until they succeed one way or another. If they discover that a project is a "three-legged horse", they "shoot it" rather than race it. Wealth creation can never be achieved without encountering extraordinary roadblocks, setbacks, and failures. These can only be overcome through creative persistence.

Take Action

a. State a dream to practice vision mapping skills on.

b. State the broad ramifications of achieving that dream.

c. Make a list of the people that you want to share your vision with.

d. List the potential obstacles that could prevent you from achieving that dream.

e. For each potential obstacle, develop creative alternatives for overcoming the obstacle.

f. List your weaknesses, "lack of know-how", and "lack of resources" that could prevent you from achieving that dream.

g. List the types of partners, mentors, or outside resources you will need to recruit to overcome the limitations you've defined.

h. Review all of your target dates for achieving your important dreams and consider if they should be revised to follow a marathoner's pace or a sprinter's pace. Any long-term vision may require a long-term commitment and therefore may need a marathoner's pace with extended deadlines.

2. Make a list of some of your past failures, both at home and on the job and when you started a new business. Consider each one and determine if you were trying to run a "three-legged horse", or if you simply failed because of your "lack of resources", "lack of know-how", or inability to develop creative alternatives.

3. List some of the failures that people around you (at home or at work or your peers) have experienced and write down your response or reaction to those failures. Did you lecture, advise, criticize, discipline, overcorrect, or become angry?

Or, did you listen, encourage, ask questions and coach the person through their "strikeout"? How could you have better dealt with their failures?

Ask yourself if you are trying to achieve those vision mapping tasks at a "sprinter's pace" or a "marathoner's pace". You may need to move some of your target dates back in order to move into the "marathoner's pace". *Any important dream is likely to require a long-term commitment, and that means establishing a steady, reliable pace for the long haul.*

PERSONAL POWER

Personal power is power that is intrinsic to the person who has it. The greater the destiny that you have, the greater the demand is going to be put on your life, your personal capacity. Your personal capacity is the sum total of your spiritual, emotional, mental, physical, relational and financial resources that you can invest in the battle or climb up to the summit of your calling. Your mountain of me has to be fully occupied for you to dispossess the strongman in the area of your calling. The mountain of me is your wheel of life.

The wheel of life can be split into ten areas - you can use 6 to 8 areas:

1. Spiritual;

2. Emotional;

3. Marriage/Romance;

4. Family/Friends;

5. Fun/Recreation;

6. Home/Work Environment;

7. Personal Growth;

8. Health/Appearance;

9. Career;

10. Financial.

Love holds all things and all the components together.

If the wheel is not filled out and functioning, you will have a rocky ride on your way to convergence. The enemy and life will hit you where you are weak and strong (strength over-extended becomes a weakness); life will explore all weakness and if you don't take care of all your capacity, the tyre you are neglecting is the one that will blow out when you reach career capacity and potentially pull you out of convergence. With the wheel of life, I look at convergence and other nuisances in the 10 sections as they are all connected. The kind of friends you want to create room are friends that stimulate growth and friends stimulating the person you want to be.

Some friends give total and unconditional acceptance (TUA) but are not helping you grow. As you have so much time, energy and resources you will have to gradually cut down on communication with some people to make room for new people. For us to remain creative and resourceful we need both ebb and flow. To use the wheel, there are several questions to ask. One of them is: Do you know how to dial down and hit the reset button? *How much we know ourselves is extremely important; how we treat ourselves is more important.* To have any level of fulfilment in life and create long-term wealth you need balance and strength in a few key foundational areas of:

- Health;
- Finance; and
- Relationships.

They are like a three-legged chair where if one leg is out of place, the rest will really suffer. Moving on from the 10-part wheel of life, for wealth creation, I will use the following building blocks of Thought, Spirit, Soul, Body, Finance, Social, Vocation, Charity and Hope.

Thought

Everything we say and do does not happen in a random vacuum, as we think before we speak. If you don't think deeply about what you want to achieve, about your dreams or desire every day, you will not operate at level 10. Your dream has to be a hunger. Thoughts are real - they occupy mental real estate. Every thought has a "heart" - the intention of that thought. God looks at this 'heart' (Jeremiah 17:10) to give to each man according to his ways and according to the results of his deeds.

Essentially it is naive for us to think that any thought we accommodate is harmless - no thought is harmless. To elaborate a bit, you can't have a negative thought about someone and smile at them sweetly and think your real thoughts are not going to be transmitted.

> *"And the Lord said, Behold, the people is one, and they have all one language; and this they begin to do: and now nothing will be restrained from them, which they have imagined to do."* (Genesis 11:6)

The science of this scripture is that as we are thinking we are physically building substance, and whatever is substance in your brain you will act upon. God has designed us to be entangled in each other's life; what this means is that your thoughts are impacting your spirit, soul and body, the people in your immediate environment and also people that are thousands of miles away. If there is a toxic thought of bitterness or unforgiveness embedded in your soul against someone thousands of miles away, you are impacting your life and theirs. Or if, for example, you watch someone eat your favourite meal, and you were hungry, the same areas in your brain will light up as the person eating the meal - there is no distance limitation in the realm of thought.

Quantum physics actually explains this in terms of the theory of entanglement which means we are all connected to each other's lives. So we feel each other's emotions. You can't hide an attitude because of the design of the brain. Everything we say and do does not happen in a random vacuum. God has designed us with mirror neurons in our brain. Only God and you know your exact thought; however, as a man thinks so he is. If your thoughts are based on lies we will manifest that lie; it is the same case for thoughts based on the absolute truth, not just the tradition and philosophy of men.

"Our life is what our thoughts make it" - Marcus Aurelius

When you are around someone that is joyful you feel great because our attitudes rub off on each other. Every thought you build generates electromagnetic energy and produces a state of mind, and it is part of non-verbal communication as the attitude comes through. We have all sort of structures in our brain that help us reflect each other's emotions; for example, the vagus nerve, insula and mirror nerve cells of our brain help us to play, cry and work together. Every single cell in our body is impacted by a negative thought - the thought will come out even when not spoken. Aggressive thoughts about others reduce the healing property of the body considerably. It's also important we are aware that stuff does pass through the generations. The decision that your great-great-grandparents made are in your head and when we are not using our minds (intellect, will and emotions) to listen to what the Holy Spirit lays down in the depths of our spirit, we may be listening to the lies of the enemy. Whatever we listen to, we will think about and whatever we think about grows into a physical thought, with its' 'heart' being reflected in our attitude. People pick up on our attitudes - the intent of the thought - not the detail of the thought. Reflecting our 'hearts' is how God designed us.

Use your God-given brain in the way it was intended by thinking the thoughts of God to the point that your spirit, soul and body are working as one supernatural unit. God is love, and we are made in His image. Our minds and our brains operate at peak efficiency when they work in love. Man's brain is wired to operate in God's love.

We are designed to think well, choose well and build healthy thoughts. We have to learn fear - it's not a natural response. If we make wrong choices, we actually create brain damage, and that creates chaos in our brains. We were created perfect; we can renew our minds - our thoughts can be brought in line with God's pattern and Word. At a fundamental level we are wired for God's love; when we align and connect to what God tells us to do, then we will think correctly and our brains will do what they are supposed to do.

You have the power of God at your disposal to command your mind as to what to think, what to say and what to do. You have control. Our brain is what our mind uses to direct our emotions and body to work together properly. When toxic thoughts come, take responsibility and refuse those thoughts. If we don't refuse toxic thoughts, we will have chosen to add imperfect programming to our minds. A corrupt mind will produce a corrupt brain and conscience that, in turn, will corrupt the whole being (spirit, soul and body). With the power of the Holy Spirit, you can choose to bring recovery to your mind and brain using His Word.

You are transformed by the Word of God — be transformed by the renewing of your mind. You have to make the decision to change your mind - to purge yourself - and to do those things that God has already said to do.

Uniquely Made, Uniquely You

The brain has seven different pillars that go all the way through the entire brain. We all have the same pillars and the same brain structure. How we use those seven pillars of thought produces our uniqueness. When you use all seven pillars in a God-designed and designated way, your gift will be in operation, and you'll be thinking clearly. A thought has to go through all seven pillars for you to build a thought properly. They all work together. Learning is a result of thinking. Each of the seven pillars is responsible for a specific type of thinking.

The Seven Pillars of Thinking

A. Intrapersonal - governs the thought interacts with your core values.

B. Interpersonal - determines how the thought affects your relationships.

C. Words spoken and written - verbalize the thought.

D. Logical/mathematical - tries to understand the thought logically.

E. Kinaesthetic - applies movement to the thought as necessary.

F. Musical - attempts to understand all facets of the thought using intuition.

G. Visual/Spatial - through imagination, "sees" the thought with your mind's eye.

Your uniqueness comes from how you use these pillars of thinking and how long you spend in each zone.

Choice and Free Will

Choice is free will - most of our actions are pre-programmed. As you think, the grains of your brain form words into physical thoughts made of proteins - what we think about affects all the cells in our body. We think, feel and then choose. As we choose we cause genetic expression and physical change in our body. Thinking always lead to a choice. Thinking and choosing are controlled by us. We were created to have love, power and a sound mind as our default. Fear and love can't co-exist. We build thoughts through our choices - choose life. We never process everything the first time we hear a message or a concept; our brain is designed to hear things over and over again to get more out of it. We never get the full benefit of a message or teaching if we only listen once. Science is God stuff. We understand God through science. We are choosing all the time the moment we are awake. God says I understand you. Do you understand you?

There are two realities we can live in called the 'love zone' and the 'fear zone'. We are made in God's image and God is love. The love zone is the truth, the reality. The love zone is the perfect zone for you. The fear zone is when we step out of our perfect zone. Love and fear are two opposite spiritual forces; they cannot coexist. We are either operating on normal and natural which is the love zone, or we have stepped out of our love zone (which is the perfectly you zone), into the non-perfectly you zone - the fear zone. We do this through our choices, the way we think.

Spirit

You are designed for the Holy Spirit to lead your spirit, your spirit to lead your soul and your soul to lead your body. Worshipping God creates a whole network in your brain to help fight negative stress and protect your memory.

Our spirit is the highest part of us; it has our intuition, wisdom, conscience and communion. Our intuition is where the Holy Spirit lays down the truth. Our communion is where our desire to worship and join up with God sits. We were made for relationship with God. The spirit of man connects to the body of man through the soul. Our soul has our intellect, will, mind and emotions. Thinking, feeling and choosing, happen in the dominion of the soul. As we consciously live we are thinking, choosing and feeling. There is a consequence for our choices - we fail to see this when we don't connect the dots and understand that the spirit, soul and body are integrated. I pursue a constant internal dialogue with the Holy Spirit because when I do this I will choose well.

There is a DNA you carry that links to your destiny. God has hidden this treasure in a place where nobody else can steal it and perhaps in the one place you never thought to look - inside yourself! Your spirit carries the DNA code to your calling, purpose, and destiny. If you are a believer you have what's called a "regenerated" spirit, or a "born again" spirit man. A whole, new, you, is living inside of you. This new spirit has your spiritual DNA!

Years ago, I was troubleshooting a problem with my colleague in the office; it was a technology issue that had a service level agreement where we only had 24 hours left to resolve the issue. The context is I wanted to resolve the issue before I could go home, else my company would pay a fine. After we spent over 3 hours troubleshooting, I told my colleague that I needed to take a break. So I went into the kitchen to have a conversation with the Holy Ghost. The conservation took about 5 minutes. In fact, I got counsel from the Holy Spirit on what to do to solve the issue. When I got back to the work area I told my colleague what we had to do (I didn't tell him what I did in the kitchen) and, to cut the long story short, my concept solved the problem; in other words, the Holy Spirit made me look like a guru. Four years later my colleague still called me an expert and I just smiled at him. If I had known the answer I would not have wasted more than 3 hours going back and forth. *The spirit realm is the causal realm and the Holy Ghost has all the answers. The Holy Spirit gives life.* The spirit realm can be split into three broad categories:

a. The Holy Spirit and His angel;

b. Human spirits;

c. The Devil, his fallen angels and his demons (the devil and his group introduced and sustain lawlessness, sickness, iniquity and sin in the world).

God is LOVE and God loves you. Lucifer hates everything that God loves. The enemies we face are not of flesh and blood; they are invisible spirit beings. Lucifer's ambition is to elevate himself to a position of equality with God. Flattery, fear and lies are Lucifer's way of doing things. Practically, Lucifer is too evil to listen to. From the moment of man's creation, Lucifer saw him as a rival to eliminate. Lucifer overflows with pride, however, whoever humbles himself will be exalted, whoever exalts himself will be humbled. The synopsis is the Devil has LEGITIMATE AUTHORITY over all those who are in rebellion against GOD. Satan is excellent with trading, business and commerce in a corrupt way. Lucifer has been a persistent trader for thousands of years and we can learn lessons about persistence and how he maintains a fine-tuned offensive army.

> *"Your heart was lifted up because of your beauty; you corrupted your wisdom for the sake of your splendour. You defiled your sanctuaries by the multitude of your iniquities, by the iniquity of your trading."*
> (Ezekiel 28:17-18)

When Satan receives worship, to him it affirms his claim to be equal with GOD. God offers a way out of Satan's kingdom and into God's kingdom. Satan accuses us day and night; his sole purpose is to prove us guilty. For those who believe and accept Jesus Christ and the power of the Cross, the guilt of Adam is no longer held against them; the gospel of Christ is the only hope for a confused and messed-up world.

> *"For the message of the cross is foolishness to those who are perishing, but to us who are being saved it is the power of God."* (1 Corinthians 1:18)

Soul

We will prosper and be in health even as our soul prospers. A prosperous soul makes you get up and fight for stuff that is important to you. Some people carry an expectation of rescue: "take me out of this pain or pressure." We need to fight through our issues; we need to be persistent. The poverty spirit makes you lie down or low. The condition of the soul is connected to every part of life - a wounded soul will cause financial ruin, divorce, destroyed relationships, impacts children and the list goes on. Soul prosperity is key to having an abundant life. One of the things I like to do is to help people get healed and delivered of their soul wounds. To build a prosperous soul we need to keep renewing our mind, will, intellect and emotions in the love zone and not in the fear zone and this will help us address root lies.

The brain can be changed through stimulation and meditation. The choices we have made and the things that have happened to us will have been processed into the brain. The brain stores our experiences and informs our reaction to those things. We have the ability to exhibit our experiences through our brains. We can achieve massive resourcefulness if we use our mind correctly.

You can change your brain with your mind. What's on your mind?

Use your God-given brain in the way it was intended by thinking the thoughts of God to the point that your spirit, soul and body are working as one supernatural unit. A sound mind is a mind of love and power. If your mind is fear-driven and fear-controlled, it's not a sound mind. Faith comes by hearing, and that's a process (Romans 10:17). When you hear something physically, it goes into your short-term memory for 24 to 48 hours. If you continue to think about it for at least three days, you have the beginning of a memory. Every day that you think about something, you strengthen the thought until you have built a long-term memory. If you continue to think about and use it for 63 days or more, it becomes a habit.

If nothing changes in the realm of your habits, nothing will change in the realm of the results.

Habits

Beliefs

Results

Each person is a gift of God and we should not envy anyone. We should celebrate who we are, and who they are. We must recognize the unique, individual nature of each person. Our minds are designed to be unique, therefore we think differently from each other. Everyone is fearfully and wonderfully made. Our intelligence continues to develop throughout our lives. IQ tests and personality profiles limit our understanding of our intelligence and uniqueness. One of my wellness mentors, Dr Caroline Leaf, developed theories that teach the ways in which we are unique, and how our minds can change our brains. We are unique in how we process information and discipline our thought life.

A thought is a memory - it takes 63 days to build a stable memory. A memory is an implantation (planting a seed). We can implant toxic memories, that will cause chaos or good memories, that lead to a healthy body, good decisions and a good life, though it's through the conscious mind that you make changes in your thinking. When we meditate on the Word of God, a memory comes up from the non-conscious mind to help us understand current thoughts and information received from the five physical senses. The conscious mind reconceptualises and redesigns the memory, or the thought, to match the Word of God; therefore, your mind is being renewed.

Toxic thoughts combined with toxic choices bring chaos to the brain. Memory loss comes from one of three types of damage to the brain including:

- Bad choices – voluntary damage to the brain;
- Trauma – involuntary damage to the brain; and
- Unhealthy chemicals and diet.

You can control your reactions that will determine the health of your mind, brain, body and spiritual development. If you misuse your mind, your brain and body will suffer. When you listen to the Holy Spirit, you have the almighty power of God moving through your mind that positively affects your brain. Allowing offense to be rooted in your soul will cause a lot of havoc. Some offenses and wounds are transferred through the generations. The Holy Spirit can heal you of offense that came through sin or trauma.

When it comes to the soul 'the best defence is no offence', else you give the enemy a legal ground against your destiny and he will just borrow your mind and use it for his own agenda.

It's true, sometimes, that it's super difficult not to be offended. But in all seriousness, offense is a sin that will wound your soul and then eventually cause you to be sick! I once had a conversation with a classmate, and he said something like, "I will never forgive James." Then I thought for a moment and my response was something like, 'Have you factored the cost of not forgiving till you die? Apart from the soul wound, then the bitter root it will create in your soul, ultimately you are sinning against yourself no matter what anyone has done to you if you refuse to forgive. At the end of the day, un-forgiveness is a sin and the wages of sin is death, but the gift of God is eternal life in Christ.'

Our thoughts and emotions impact our health and wealth. To change your mindset, the mind needs a focus, a mentor and an instruction.

Focus which will be a vision, an expected end state, and your vision mentors you. If your vision does not scare you, you need to change it. The voice you choose to listen to mentors you. Hearing God mentoring you is key to have clarity and wisdom. It is difficult to hear the voice of God if you are not focusing on His presence, intimacy and relationship with Him. Decide what you want to experience every day. *Your habits are vehicles.* They will take you into a desirable or undesirable future. What you are doing today is creating a permanent you. Schedule your pleasure because pain will schedule itself.

Body

Our physical health and energy have to be managed; statistics show lifestyle diseases are very common in both developed and undeveloped countries. A majority of physical illnesses happen because of poor diet, poor exercise, toxicity and nutritional deficiency. Research shows that unless you eat mindfully, thinking correctly before during and after eating, you won't give your body the correct nutrition - eating is 80% thinking! Mindful eating keeps the weight off and nourishes the mind, brain and body. Indeed, our global food production system is deeply flawed. Fortunately, it is possible for us to vote with "our thoughts and forks" for better practices that respect our health and the health of the planet.

As a generation, we are exposed to toxicity inside and outside. The skin is the largest organ in the body and can be exposed to 500 chemicals per day, especially among women that use a lot of beauty products which have toxins. We need to make better health, exercise and diet choices for long-term physical endurance. It is not just about cutting carbs and increasing proteins; it is not one size fits all. The discipline we need is the discipline required to make these choices a habit. While understanding that different body types require different diet types and exercise plans, a toxin-free body and a healthy human soul lays the foundation for true health before adding other building blocks like diet types, exercise plans and supplements.

The main signals that your cells respond to are your thoughts. Think in a wholesome manner and see things from God's perspective. Our 75 to 100 trillion cells each contain the full DNA complement. Each cell has about 1,000 "receptors" or "doorways" on the outside, designed to open at specific times to receive what they need. If things in our brains are not working correctly, the "doors" on the receptors will rip off, and there will be cell chaos. When we think toxic thoughts, our genetic expression explodes in a negative way. When someone has years and years of responding negatively to life's events and circumstances, the brain cells' receptors are open to various diseases - they will have put themselves in the vulnerable zone.

Shift Your Brain into Super Position

It is possible to lead an emotionally happy and physically healthy lifestyle by simply learning to control your thought life. You can begin the journey of mind renewal by the Word of God and switch on your brain to victory. When you are obedient to God's instructions, you are empowered to have strength; therefore, you can direct your memory, your words and your brain toward His thoughts. The instructions you receive from God's Word have a large, positive effect on your brain. Every time you choose God's way, you begin operating in superpower thinking, in good decision making, you make the right decisions, and your brain sends the correct signals throughout your body so that God's life is built in you. When you choose God's way, His energy that comes directly from the throne of grace fills your mind and body (Hebrews 4:16). Choosing God brings health, life, longevity, healing and change.

Hope

Hope is the desired and expected end. The word "hope" from a heavenly perspective means a joyful expectation of good; it's the ability to see the unseen realm. Hope allows us to see the unseen; when we can see from God's perspective of what is around us, we actually have hope. It creates a picture of what God wants to do. It does not take a special gift, but it takes a perspective shift.

Just as faith protects our hearts, hope protects our mind.

One thought from Heaven can change everything for you if it is followed through. I have had several God thoughts that I knew were not mine and, sometimes, it happened in the most unexpected places. One thought from God can give us an idea to reach a new market and to reach people in our region or cultures we never thought possible.

We need to protect our hope for the future and our generations. I have a hope that spans over 200 years. We need the helmet of hope - its primary purpose is to protect our mind - our thought life. The devil has a mind and so do the minions of malicious spirits that do his bidding. Their task is to penetrate your thought life. The helmet is referred to as a helmet of 'hope' in 1 Thessalonians 5. This could be described as the supernatural ability to keep a tightly insulated thought life against all intruding toxic thoughts and faith-robbing negativity. Individuals who keep their helmets firm have trained themselves to avoid self-sabotaging self-talk as they partner with God in His plans and promises for their present, future and nations. I live with a 200-year plan for my descendants and the continent of Africa as the thrust. *"For I will pour out water on the thirsty land and streams on the dry ground; I will pour out My Spirit on your offspring, and My blessing on your descendants"* (Isaiah 44:3).

What are some ways you can prevent self-sabotage?

Record. You would be surprised at how many sacred moments occur in a 24-hour period. You will discover the significance of these experiences by making it a habit to review them at the end of the day. I have a journal I carry everywhere. I encourage you to get a journal and take time to record these daily miracles as reference experiences for when you're encountering a new challenge. *Too frequently, we miss those God-moments that, whether they seem large or small, are truly sensational.*

Rehearse. Remind yourself of who God is. Look upon the whole of your life and one word about God will stand out - His faithfulness! Replay every victory you've ever had before you make a critical decision. Do this on purpose because if you're not careful, without a helmet to intercept them, you'll start replaying the tape of what has *gone wrong* in the past. *If you yield to negative thinking, you'll focus on what went wrong. This will sabotage the results you want to see.*

Pre-play. The brain is a captivating thing. *Under the helmet of hope, you actually can protect your thoughts from self-sabotaging by pre-playing what God wants to do in the future.* This is possible by loading up your thought life with times when things went brilliantly. Your imagination is a tool given by God. Use it to rehearse what you believe God wants to do. Mental rehearsal is the discipline of Olympic champions and miracle workers alike. *Keep a visual image of what you're aiming for - the outcome the Bible promises. Do this and watch what happens.*

Personal Finance

Here we will deal with the Belief System/Mindset and the Hard Look.

Belief System/Mindset

I have dealt with some people in financial trouble and found out as time has gone on, that education helps very little when the people are unable to learn. Though people have financial pain and want breakthrough, they will not change as long as information is presented at a skill level instead of a heart understanding level. I have seen that sharing the latest tricks and techniques cannot effect change until the knowledge moves from mind to heart. These people want relief from financial pain, but pain evasion is no match for a deeply held belief, especially if that belief is a lie.

Whenever there is an internal belief that contradicts rational skills, the lesson will fail until the contradiction is resolved. No matter how irrational the belief or how exceptional the skill, this unfortunate fact remains true. Conflict in the heart always results in behaviour that follows what is deeply trusted. In the case of money and wealth, every internal belief manifests around you. Identify any financial conflict with money, or you'll see that no real long-term change happens until the conflict is resolved. In the end, I observe that money issues are not really about money but about the belief systems operating within the heart.

We could look at belief system in relation to finances in three broad categories: the poor, the middle class and the wealthy.

From our belief system, we fulfil our prophecies. A lot of the poverty you see in the west is self-inflicted. For something important to them, the poor think, "I have no money"; they say "I can't afford it"; they feel vulnerable; they look for handouts; they expect lack and struggle and external help; their destiny is just about survival.

The middle class thinks I work for money; they say I can't afford it on my credit card; they feel entitlement and competition; they feel like they deserve something and are sometimes in competition with their peers or neighbours.

The wealthy will say "how can I afford it"; they will find a way; they have a willingness to work towards a goal; The wealthy think, "Money works for me, I don't work for money"; they think, "I can afford it", according to a plan because they are not cost sensitive. If you aim at nothing you are sure to hit nothing. They expect endless opportunities. The wealthy are dreaming how I can help someone, build a giving organization that will build a mountain of strength. In the earning cycles, the wealth of the poor does not grow, it is just for subsistence. The middle class is an economic engine that works and get raises, their net worth (assets after their debts are paid off) grows and falls. As a group the middle class does not know how to hang on to their wealth - they gain it and lose it over a long span of time; you see a family that does not go that far financially.

The wealthy have a different experience; they know how to hold onto their wealth when they gain it. The gain is normal for both the middle class and the wealthy and it is the blessing of the Lord. However, the earning cycle of the wealthy increases exponentially because of multiple streams of income and multiplication. We need to know how to manage and protect what we are doing. When wealth is lost it does not evaporate, it goes to someone else who can be, for example, a banker, but it ultimately ends up in the hands of the wealthy who know how to extract wealth. When you can't hang onto your wealth it goes away to someone who can. Wealth can be built through concentration and specialization on one asset class; it can be protected through diversification into various assets that are not uncorrelated.

Dominion is having a perspective that God is always bringing blessings and multiplication to you. Poverty is not fun - from Heaven's perspective, the poor are unproductive.

Wisdom Keys:

A. Go after the root lies;

B. You get what you pay for;

C. If it is too good to be true, it needs to be investigated further;

D. Calm seas don't make good sailors;

E. There are economic cycles. When a cycle turns down you have to figure out a different type of opportunity. Plan accordingly - don't be shocked, it's been happening for centuries;

F. Don't invest in what you can't explain;

G. Haste leads to poverty;

H. If you have not bumped into greed you have not had a big enough opportunity;

I. Be careful and shrewd. A man with money meets a man with experience. After they meet the man with money, they leave with the experience and the man with experience leaves with the money;

J. Seize the wheel and live within your means;

L. Living within your means as a long-term model is a pathway to gain wealth.

Money is measured in time. Realise when you are selling your time as an employee. Your time is spent working, and at the end of that pay period, you take your pay cheque or pay in your account - it is an inventory of that time.

If you consume half of the money on your rent and other stuff to live, and the rest of it is sitting in the bank, you have now inventoried time. If you lose a job or contract, a measure of wealth is to answer this question: 'how long can I survive without that stream of income from the contract'? And when I look at one of my little bank accounts and it says £XX000.00, I have just a very little bit of wealth in that account compared to my responsibilities. I have a little bit of time inventoried in that account. In other words, when you save a huge chunk or accumulate a large amount of money on earth or in heaven, you have a shelf full of time and your job became optional.

The Hard Look

This is where you take a hard look at the facts and not distort them. Am I on the path or not? Take a hard look at the numbers. To do this we need to do the calculation that yields.

- Full month expense Journal/ Discovery
- Balance State/net worth
- Income statement

Discovery

Figure out where we are on the map. I have had people write down every expense item they did for an entire month in a document called an expense journal. It is a good exercise for the bold. if you don't have a working budget, the expense journal is a good place to start if you want the hard look at facts; however, if you hide stuff from the expense journal because you don't want the financial planner to know or whoever you are accountable to, it defeats the purpose. You have to be honest with yourself and look. For example, when you train as a pilot, it is important to know how to read your dials. Some pilots can fly in the pitch black of night - these kinds of pilots are trained to obey and follow their dials. Flying at night by following our dials applies the same way when it comes to operating with our finance. Money moves so fast, it moves at the speed of thoughts - especially out of the chequebook. When you operate in your finance, it is always at night, visibility is always zero. You have to learn how to function based on your dials.

Your dials are the balance sheet and the income statement.

At a minimum, you have to raise your financial know-how, to understand what balance sheets and income statements are because we are flying when it comes to our money, and it is always at night where your intuition may wreck you. This will be proved by your history. Your chequebook is your history. Your chequebook will show you what you believe and value. With money, the wealthy have intent not intuition. They design their plan (budget), they lay out the flight plan. The budget is nothing but a plan, a laid-out intention to whatever your goals are.

Another item is net worth - it is a function of your balance sheet. A balance sheet is a list of everything you own (including all the things on our assets list) minus a list of everything you owe (including mortgage) giving you a net worth. Asset minus debt is your net worth (assets include money in accounts and certificates of deposit). This gives you the hard look. Debt is everything you owe including pledges, investments loans (leverage).

Net worth = total asset – total debt

Risk and return follow each other - savings accounts in banks are federally insured, that is why you get about 1% interest. The government guarantees you get your money back provided the country does not go belly up. Liquidity is good for you, but not for the bank. A higher risk venture needs higher returns to justify it.

Income Statement

Income statement affluent is someone who has a lot of earning potential and can go out and borrow based on their capacity to pay the debt. They buy good cars, clothes, the best shoes, based on the amount of money flowing through their pipe. This is different to balance sheet affluent. The wealthy watch their balance sheet (net worth) to determine if they are flying and tracking in the right direction, the right way. The middle class tend to watch their income statement - they are affluent based on the income statement, not their balance sheet.

Debt is bondage, especially when you can't profit from it. Most consumer debts people acquire due to their lifestyle, good (investment) debt or bad debts, have a degree of bondage when one lender has overwhelming control and leverage over the borrower.

The income statement is based on cash flows; it is how much is coming in vs. how much is going out. For example, a Medical Doctor (Physician) may have a big pipe and a lot more money flowing through it when compared to someone that works in a Starbucks store who has a smaller pipe. Nonetheless, they both have jobs, and there is money flowing through.

A person who has a lot of earning potential will go out and borrow money based on their capacity to pay the debt. They become income statement affluent - they can buy big cars, cool stuff, and have the best shoes; their nails are always done and their lifestyle is based on the amount of money flowing through their pipe. The problem is they tend to spend all the money they get, so over a long period of time, most of their wealth is own by somebody else. Income Statement affluence over a long period of time generates income for their lenders. In other words, they are an economic engine for someone else who has invested in them - usually the bankers or lenders.

If I am income statement affluent I can look really good and I can be generous, but I may not really be growing wealth. The balance sheet affluent are different - they are watching their net worth. They have a different agenda going on - they watch their net worth grow. It is a different mind-set. The formula below is a good place to start to see if you are balance sheet or income statement affluent:

Take your age X Annual Income X 0.112 = Expected Net Worth

The 0.112 is a factor that was created and presented by Thomas Stanley in the book "The Millionaire Mind". The answer to the formula should equal your net worth.

The income statement is less valuable or inferior to the balance statement when we are measuring wealth. However, the income statement is a powerful tool; it measures your economic engine/motor. How much money is going out is a measure of your lifestyle; if you do the concept of "living within your means", if you spend less than you bring in and control your appetite as a long-term model, you will gain wealth. We go through sessions where we live beyond our means, like when we go through university, but don't let living beyond your means become your plan.

Have a budget and don't see the budget as a restraint, see it as an enabler, as a plan and a strategy to get what you want and for reaching your first dreams. When you build your plan on purpose and work it out, your budget is no longer a constraining thing anymore, it becomes an enabler.

Take your financial life and divide it into five categories:

- Living;
- Giving;
- Saving;
- Debt Service; and
- Legacy.

Living: What does it cost me to live including housing, food, and haircut, etc.?

Giving: I believe in the tithe, monthly first fruits, alms...

Saving: Match your saving to your giving (Challenge)

If you are a generous giver, I challenge you to match your giving to your saving (you don't have to). As an example, if you give 15% and save 15% you are automatically forced to live on less than 70%, which means you are living below your means. We can make money complicated. Seize the wheel. Once you have what you need, stop increasing your standard of living if you want to grow wealth. If you do this, your disposable income will increase as the pot and economic motor will get bigger and stronger because you are controlling the outflow of the pipe. Over time the economic engines then become the source for doing some of your dreams. The dreams become little buckets of the storehouse. A storehouse builder can give away strength and life; if you are not living within your means you can't be a storehouse builder. A store builder needs wisdom, to multiply the storehouses.

Emergency Funds

Becoming the bank, this is like a bumper in your airbag. When you have an emergency fund you don't need to go to the credit card when the car blows a tyre or when a major repair comes as you have become the bank. By becoming the bank your economic strength will gain momentum and seize. With EF you pay yourself instead of the lender.

One question that I ask is 'How big should your EF be'? It depends on how much time you need in your life and how much of a bumper you need. It is going to be different for somebody just starting out versus someone who has children. Remember wealth is measured in time. How much is enough?

Debt Assault

There are a lot of great websites on how to get out of debt. The debt snowball and debt avalanche are two approaches to paying off all of your debt.

Debt snowball – A payoff method that pays off your smallest debt first.

Debt avalanche –The debt payoff method that saves the most money in interest. When it comes to paying off debt, you may have heard a hundred pieces of advice. Stop investing while you pay it off, start with the smallest balance or start with the highest interest rate, consolidate your debt or don't consolidate your debt. The science says that humans aren't really rational creatures. I will use the debt avalanche approach if I had several debts to pay since it is the rational thing to do and mathematically this is the most effective way to eliminate debt. Furthermore, this is Thomas Stanley's conclusion after studying 1000 millionaires:

You cannot enjoy life if you are addicted to consumption and the use of credit.

When someone is addicted to consumption and the use of credit as a habit, they are surely living beyond their means - except they don't earn enough to live on.

What we need more is true riches: 'Desire fulfilled is a tree of life'.

Social, Vocation & Charitable

Social: How you build inspiring social and business networks.

"You are the average of the five people you spend the most time with" - Jim Rohn[1]

Vocation: This is where and how you deliver your ultimate service, how you discover your unique skills and talent and take it to the world with your unique expression to fulfil your ultimate purpose. You are a company of unique skills and talents.

Charitable: This is the realm of giving and doing what helps people - one of them is by distributing wealth and giving because you want to:

1. Meet a human need;
2. Support a charity;
3. Honour.

When done properly there is a link between giving, prayer and the miraculous.

"Now there was a man at Caesarea named Cornelius, a centurion of what was called the Italian cohort, a devout man and one who feared God with all his household, and gave many alms to the Jewish peo-

---

1. http://www.goodreads.com/author/show/657773.Jim_Rohn

ple and prayed to God continually. About the ninth hour of the day he clearly saw in a vision an angel of God who had just come in and said to him, "Cornelius!" And fixing his gaze on him and being much alarmed, he said, "What is it, Lord?" And he said to him, "Your prayers and alms have ascended as a memorial before God." (Acts 10:1-4 New American Standard Bible (NASB))

In the realms of philanthropy when your motive is right, long-term wealth is strengthened by philanthropy. Philanthropy is based on two Greek words which mean 'loving' and 'people'. When you give money or time to a charity after your due diligence, you may not get something back technically or tangibly immediately; the value you get in return is that you know broken people have been taken care of and lives have been transformed. The people you are helping may not have the resource to return value for value, but you are doing a service because you love people. If we understand what is going on we will be naturally generous.

SIGHT, SOUND AND LIGHT

SIGHT

When your seeing is incomplete your saying will be incomplete; when we get dull in our seeing our sayings dries up, and we begin to conform to the atmosphere around us. The filter system in our souls can be blurred based on what we have been through - this most times will give us a perception that is the opposite of the truth. It is common to see fear-based perception that has been ingrained as the truth. If you have an offense in your soul and you get a revelation about your future, there will potentially be a wrong interpretation of how to progress into this future because the offense will have missed up your filter system.

To illustrate this point, look at an object around you. What do you see? On one dimension the object is reflecting light, which allows your eyes and brain to process a mental real estate for the object and also to form the communication required to describe the object. Behind the object, there are movements, which constitute 'the what' and 'the who' of the object. It will be inappropriate to just see the object in one dimension. Look at a table around you as an example, in the higher dimension.

You will notice that physical matter is nothing more than the swirling of electrons, quakes, protons ... It's really the gathering together of invisible factors at various levels of density. You will see that utterance is the driving force that created a material universe and is the input for the tree manifesting. What holds it together according to Colossians, is the word of His (God's) power that created physical matter. The word of his power holds it together in its composition. You will see that the difference in the tree and the table is *processing* - one is a process, i.e. a raw state, the other is the outcome, i.e. a finished product.

We are in a time to triumph and all around you, you will see the Light moving - these are his angels and God is offering you an upgrade that will create transformation when you embrace His invitation.

If you want your external world to change, the image you see must change. Just because we don't always see the movement does not mean they are not there. It's key to appreciate that there is always a lot going on around us.

When you start to move into convergence with your purpose, your destiny, you are entering into something which has already got juice on it because God already wrote it in His book. I honestly believe that it's at that level that you start to get what I would call 'horizon line perception' or sight at an extraordinary level - meaning you have the power to tap into a clear expectation of the next course of events in your life, be they good or be they bad. You should pick up on it in the internal radar.

If you don't know your end you don't know what to say yes to; short-sightedness is when you lack 20/20 vision. We develop sight through meditation (meditating on who God has called you to be), asking questions and observing the cycles of blessings. Godly meditation is about emptying your mind so God can fill it; it is about filling it with the words of God and saying it to your own hearing until a picture is released. The picture then became a godly stronghold to stand against fear, worry, anxieties ... We will always attract our prominent thoughts.

You will reproduce what you see.

The most powerful of your five senses is *'sight'* - there is sight and then insight. The principle of imagination shows that everything we imagine is in a realm we cannot see with our physical eyes. Imagination can come from God or Satan. It is the first tool to overcoming obstacles. Leaders must develop 20/20 vision, seeing with different eyes - if you can't see it, it will not happen. People follow what they see.

- How do you see yourself? The way you see yourself is creating a world around you.
- If you don't have a picture of the end, you don't know what to say yes to and no to.
- Prophecy is a picture of the end and the Holy Spirit knows the end.

The law of Sight puts you in control so you can be happening to life, not life happening to you. The most powerful personal tool is the power of your identity - every trial you go through is asking a question: who are you?

You have to know and believe the thoughts that God has towards you and marry the truth that God has shown you, of who he has called you to be.

> *"But if your eye is bad [spiritually blind], your whole body will be full of darkness [devoid of God's precepts]. So if the [very] light inside you [your inner self, your heart, your conscience] is darkness, how great and terrible is that darkness!"* (Matthew 6:23 Amplified Bible)

SIGNATURE SOUND

We live in a voice-activated universe where everything vibrates and can respond to various frequencies. The key is the sound of your voice and when your voice is speaking what God anointed you to say in prayer, prophecy, proclamation, petition, your unique selling proposition etc., you authorize God's army (angels, chariots, horses...), to go in and open the doors of your destiny, generational blessings and purpose.

The idea of a signature sound says this: when you get into your divine purpose that is the thing that you were created to do, you are not innovating something. You aren't originating something. You are discovering that which was already scripted and written for you to enter into. In other words, you're entering into the script that was already written. Signature sound means as your thumb-print is unique in this universe from all other thumb-prints, your voice is unique from all other voices.

As the kingdom was created by utterance, the greatest untapped power you've got is the power of your signature sound.

King David, who reigned over ancient Israel in its golden age, knew in close quarter combat with thousands of occasions where death was stalking him how he evaded death, how he moved past death. Men are dying here; people are dying there. In the midst of the chaos, David eluded the process of death. One of his observations was that if he dwelt in the secret place of the Most High, he was abiding under the shadow of the Almighty and a thousand could fall at his side, ten thousand his left, and it didn't happen to him.

Why? Because he made an abiding place for himself on the inside with the spirit realm that enabled him in the material world to be able to elude traps and snares and setups and adversaries who were clearly out to destroy him. He says this about the angels. He says that they hearken. They are flames of fire sent forth to minister to the heirs of salvation. Angels are sent forth to minister to the heirs of salvation. The angels, he says, hearken unto the voice of his word.

What I want you to catch is that angels interact with the human species based on the utterance that comes out. This is why the reality of the occult if you think about it, is that demons do exist.

This whole thing about utterance I actually heard from American's top coach Tony Robbins and I thought to myself what he's saying is taken right out of the archives of what belongs to Christ. However, a religious spirit dulls the perception of the church of the marvellous, unique nature of the truth it is handling and causes it to categorise it in a way that makes it useless.

Utterance has power because when you speak, you have authority with the signature sound. Your voice is like a key that goes into the vault of the universe and opens up access to the angelic realm that was assigned for the purpose you were created to fulfil. Imagine it's a complex idea, but you were not created by accident. You were brought here by design and by time. You already ran the gamut of numerous factors in order to show up and survive.

Having said that, the signature sound you want is the sound of authenticity - you speaking what God wants coming out of your mouth so that when angels hear it, they act on that. Getting that kind of utterance is not always easy, but when you have that utterance you marshal invisible forces to your cause at a level that is completely unique compared to the competition you're up against, who are operating on their own agenda or without the blessing of God in their purpose.

Practice power-talk. Start saying what God says about your life. Words create pictures in your mind. Those pictures decide what you believe. Power-talk is simply speaking words that produce the desired result for yourself and others. Your words decide divine events in your life. Death and life are in the power of the tongue: and they that love it shall eat the fruit thereof. Your words are so powerful that they will kill or give life, and the talkative person will reap the consequences (Proverbs 18:21).

CONVERGENCE

Convergence is a phase of life where "it all starts coming together." *Convergence* happens when you do the work you were created and called to do. You enter a role that frees you to utilize 100% of your gifts, talents, and acquired skills. Convergence requires personal and career actualization. I learnt about convergence from one of my mentors, Dr Lance Wallnau.

Personal Convergence: the place where your gifts, talents and acquired skills combine with your ultimate sense of purpose - they become actualized in a role that invites you to do what you were uniquely created to do.

Career Convergence: Career Convergence is when you've personally done your homework and thus qualify to be invited to do something that Heaven itself is up to. Your heaven-sent assignment will call you to meet a need that will change the world for someone. You are going to do something that makes a difference for other people.

Career Convergence requires:

1. Your Niche in Destiny;

2. Highest and Best use of You;

3. Unique Methodology;

4. Doing/Being/Having.

The convergence stage of life taps into your power to make an ultimate contribution; in this stage of life, the leader is moved into a position that makes the fullest possible use of their experience, temperament, talent, etc. and liberates them from other activities that they are less gifted to perform. Convergence frees the leader from labour that is not best aligned with gifting. Geographic relocation and relational alignment is often (not always) an important part of convergence. The word convergence implies a coming together of certain factors in the life of a person who is fully set apart for God's purpose. When they step on the scene they impact the environment! Common characteristics of those in convergence are:

- Activity that matches a fully developed cluster of gifts, talent, and acquired skills;

- Work that aligns with life purpose;

- Unique methodology;

- Major role that liberates them to do what they do best;

- Spiritual authority gained through private victories over spiritual opposition.

Every time I see a recommended movie, I have a tendency to make comparison in my mind, pointing out how great movies resonate with great themes - and those themes are all parallels of biblical truth where there is evil trying to overcome virtue, there is somebody who represents good, somebody who represents evil, and evil is trying to overcome the good. The good guy is usually not, in the beginning, the person they become by the end of the story, because the conflict with evil shapes and brings out on the inside of them what is in them. The more spectacular the hero's potential, the more contradictions, adversities, setbacks and obstacles the hero has to go through in order to defeat the evil. These are the storylines of most great movies.

Whether that struggle is within themselves or that struggle is external, what you see is that you can measure the greatness of the hero by the magnitude of the opposition or adversary. These are all biblical themes, from darkness to life and light. We're in that story. We're on that journey. Like in the great movies to experience convergence we all go through several cycles of dreaming, distress, development and demonstration. These stages of moving in convergence and making our dream work and entail living at level 10. As we will go through several cycles of dream, distress, development and demonstration to get to level 10 living we have to be ready for the tensions when the contradictions happen.

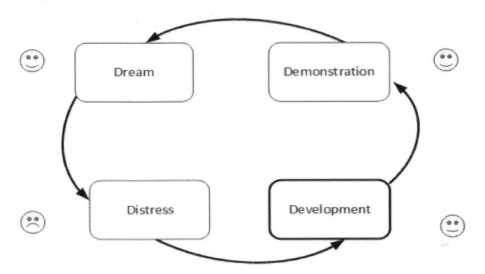

Level 10 entails doing the thing you were born to do - it's the merger of personal mastery and career mastery.

Dream	Distress	Develop	Demonstrate
Unconscious	Conscious	Conscious	Unconscious
Incompetence	Incompetence	Competence	Competence

Mastery requires:

- Doing: Time management, People, Product, Process
- Being: Living with my past, relationships, fully present
- Work: What you do best! "What can you be best in the world at?"
- Play: What you LOVE to do most! 'What energizes you? You never cease to see the beauty in this.'

Convergence is the "Being" and "Doing" of your Prophetic Destiny. Doing ... is the SCIENCE of achievement! "I glorified you. I finished the work you gave me to do" (John 17:4). BEING ... is the ART of fulfilment; I pray ye may prosper and be in health even as your soul prospers.

Understanding the Building Blocks of Convergence

- The Power of Your Scripts
- Behaviour

- Total Unconditional Acceptance (TUA)
- Thoughts and Feelings
- The Power of Your State
- Understanding Process Events
- Your Core Design

The Power of Your Scripts: The scripts you carry within - especially those scripts that define who you are. Sometimes, who you are, interferes with how you see yourself, others, and the world around you. Consequently, those deeply embedded and disempowering scripts have a profound influence on how you are likely to behave in a given circumstance. These scripts are the lenses through which you view your life.

Behaviour:

1. Behaviour is made up of the things you do.

2. Congruence occurs when you're behaving congruently with the image that God gave you.

3. When you behave congruently you are free.

Total Unconditional Acceptance (TUA): TUA is just another phrase for love. It is the unconditional love of God that enables us to be forgiven. The only way I can help other people experience this is if I have experienced this myself.

Thoughts and Feelings: Thoughts and feelings reveal what you are saying to yourself because it is impossible to feel a sustained emotion of any kind apart from the meaning you are attaching to the thing you are having strong feelings about - your scripts!

The Power of Your State:

1. Your current state reveals your self-talk, your script. Whatever you are feeling - your self-talk put you there.

2. When your deeply embedded scripts about your identity change - your whole world changes!

3. It is awareness, not perfection, that causes growth.

Understanding Process Events: A process event is the gift of a problem that when solved or resolved will increase your conformity to Christ.

Values:

1. Thoughts and feelings dictate behaviour, but values are the filter that comes before thoughts and feelings.

2. Values are made up of what you believe, what you hold dear. We desire to live congruent with our values. When behaviour threatens this, we are willing to make whatever adjustment is needed to get back to being congruent.

Your core design drives it all:

1. The heat of processing events will change you.

2. Your temperament mix is part of your core design. The values and beliefs, the life lessons and principles you're really, really working on are probably related to the way you're made.

What will change you?

1. Any strength, over-extended, becomes a weakness. Change will come when you become self-aware of the weaknesses and begin to move toward controlling your strengths.

2. Each temperament responds to different pressure points - things that move you far beyond your comfort zone and challenge you.

3. Caution: We often put more energy into avoiding the things we fear than in pursuing the things we want.

4. Once you know how you are made, you can manage yourself. When you become self-aware, you shrink the ability of your enemies to manipulate you.

5. As you practice and control your temperament and personality style, you will see positive change.

Convergence is revealed in how we behave:

Thoughts and feelings are always there. Whatever your feelings are, they're going to affect your behaviour unless you manage them.

How to Re-Frame and Shift the Moment

- When you open yourself up to what is great in this "now" moment, wisdom comes in!
- You can adjust your response any moment you are aware of it.
- Look for the patterns in your life.
- Ask, "How is this moment like my life?" By identifying patterns, you can avoid your own self-sabotaging moments.
- Mistakes you make are related to your core design. Your core design is the gift that gives you your destiny.
- When you operate in congruence, even your mistakes are teachable moments.

Convergence Zone

The *convergence zone* is something like an energy field. It is like a vortex that sucks into itself uncanny coincidences and "divine appointments."

How Do I Recognize the Convergence Zone?

Have you ever been in the middle of a conversation and you or the other person can point to goose bumps on your arm because the thing said resonated with the environment in such a way it gave you chills? This mysterious feeling is evidence of entering the *convergence zone*. It is a place where your spirit is aligned with heaven's rhythm and earth's ripple at the same time!

Here are some other aspects to help you recognize the convergence zone:

- The convergence zone is the place where you experience the future you - the person on the inside who wants to come out! You access a momentary alignment with your ultimate assignment and seem to get a glimpse of who you are in your tomorrow.

- The convergence zone is activated whenever you step into a role that fully utilizes your God-given talents.
- You have entered the convergence zone many times in your life and did not notice it. Look for clues! Reflect deeper into your childhood.

What were those electric moments for you growing up? This may have been when you performed in a play, a dance, an athletic event, participated in student council, yearbook committee, elective or election. What did you gravitate to? Who were you drawn to? Was it to people in the theatre or in music? Jocks? Intellectuals? The popular crowd? Or were you a loner? Did you prefer to hang out with your own crowd? When were you most alive? Now think about all the jobs you have ever done. What one job did you enjoy most? Why? The moments that JUMP OUT as PEAK experiences were moments you crossed through the zone. Your future was being revealed to you in those moments!

Life gives you those priceless destiny appointments so you can "taste and see" your future and confirm the direction of your calling. This is SO IMPORTANT. You need to multiply your AWARENESS and sensitivity to those moments!

You are IN the CONVERGENCE ZONE when:

- You are FEELING authentic - you are being who you really are. You have no need to wear a mask. When you are in this zone you say to yourself, "This is me. This is what I was meant to do!"
- You are 100% ALIVE because you are doing what you do best. You are energized rather than depleted by the activity.
- You lose track of time. You experience a sort of "timeless awareness." You become so fully engaged in the activity that you enter a time bubble.
- People want more. This creates more demand and experiences, which multiply more invitations and opportunities, which create more evidence of being in "the zone." *Increase, of any kind, is the signature that you are in your zone and cracking the code.*
- More opportunities create more potential for prosperity. Why?

Because you have figured out how to meet a need doing what you do best and love to do most!

LEVEL 10 LIVING

Your Paradigms and Passion

The idea that there is a future, seeking to become manifest, is one of the unique characteristics of the scriptural revelation. The nature of the prophetic is that there is something out here in the future that is calling you, now, in the present. Your worldview helps you embrace some ideas, discard others and allows you to laser focus on what God wants you to do. A lot of the impressions you have, on where you are going to be in the future is embedded here in the present. *"Where your heart is, your treasure shall be also"* (Matthew 6:21).

Ask yourself, what is it you're looking for? You need to cut off the narcissistic quest for significance and achievement that is common to all mankind. It is the one flaw in most of the success strategies I've read, because, at no point does the author ever ask "What's driving the quest for achievement? How do we sanctify that?" The Cross will sanctify how you go about pursuing your future. You need to cultivate your heart so that you develop an affection for the highest and best purpose God has for your life. A Level 10 life is a life where you can stand before Jesus and have no regrets about what you chose to do, or what you pursued, because it corresponds with the plan the Lord has for you. The real secret is when your heart is falling in love with the future God has for you.

Level 10 living is a strategic way of integrating ideas. The Lord wants to expand your character, expand your heart, so you have experiences that stretch your character capacity. God is ploughing up the foundation of your life, "the being" so that you can handle "the doing". He's also stretching your knowledge. Any time you grow, you're in territory you've never been in before. God is expanding your knowledge capacity when he gives you a problem you don't know how to solve. Your skill will be stretched, your doing will give you mastery. The gifts of the spirit expand scope of your mastery.

Your Personal Capacity in the Present

The whole arc of fulfilment isn't in the activity; the moments when you are most engaged are when you are 100% immersed in something you were doing.

It's the moment when you are transported out of yourself. You weren't multi-tasking, you were engaged with one thing. The real secret of a Level 10 activity is about total immersion in what you are doing in the moment.

Jay Stephen was working on his PhD in mathematics. He realised his career wasn't in math, so he went into mathematics in time management. His genius was helping people to understand the real secret of time management; how to enter moment by moment states of total actualisation or harmony, by getting your psychic ram free from preoccupation. The moment a subject comes up to you, you know you can download it and park it, with the absolute confidence that it will come back at the right time. This will allow you structure your days more effectively. When you structure your life such that what you do is the most important thing now (MIN), you give yourself permission for total immersion. Without total immersion you are not reaching Level 10! 10/10 requires you have total Immersion. Eden is walking in the circumference of the sphere assignment God has given us; stewarding that which the Father has given us to do right now. Make sure that your MIN is a thing that is most connected to your purpose. You must know how what you're doing applies to your purpose, to really begin. Activities like travelling to get someplace are "Necessary to Purpose" (N.P). All of your N.P. is actually assimilated into your purpose, they're part of your purpose.

Your Path

The path involves your journey to the crown, the meeting place of your high calling from God. Your path is your day-to-day decision-making - the choices you make, the things you have to do to get you from where you are to where you want to be and this takes you through a process. The crown corresponds to that process. In your life, you will have high points. Between Jesus' acts, he was revealing his ways. Gods acts are speaking for him but what is happening between those moments are processes. Jesus replied, *"You don't understand yet the meaning of what I'm doing, but soon it will be clear to you"* (John 13:7).

When we talk about the path there is a wisdom path. There are 4 stages: a dream, distress, development of your skills, knowledge and personality then finally a divine appointment for the demonstration of your gifting.

Your Power

One of the key factors in convergence, that intersection you want to move towards, where you're doing the thing you are gifted to do best, requires that you understand what your power is. Clarity is power! The clearer you are on what you do well, the easier it is to identify the people God put in your life to help you succeed by teaming up with you.

Tools like Myers Briggs, MBTI, DISC which have been used by millions, give you a unique perspective; none of them is redundant. I've done each of them and each has helped me to realise something. Each will help you identify what you do best but also what your personal constraints are. Your constraints are your strengths, overextended. Whatever it is that you've been gifted to do, could be your downfall.

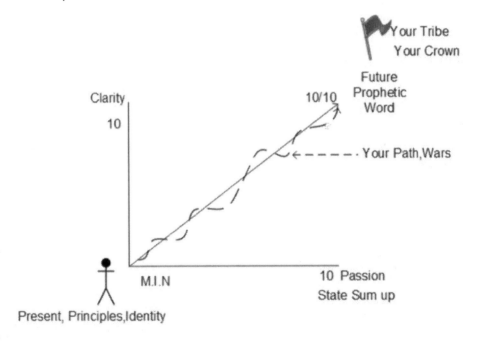

Your Prophetic Purpose

Each person on earth has a prophetic purpose. In 1 Timothy 1:18, Paul wrote to Timothy saying, "*This charge I commit unto thee, son Timothy, according to the prophecies which went before on thee, that thou by them mightest war a good war-*

fare;" What Paul is saying on our Level 10 world is that God has certain things for us in the future, according to the prophetic word that came before you. God will give you explanations regarding the future that you are called to manifest, that word will be tapped into so that you can see and hear what that future is. Your pathway may zig-zag but put this prophetic word as the true north for your compass. I love how Paul says it's a warfare. Because God has a prophetic purpose for you, the enemy is going to show up in various places along the way, to keep you from accessing the blueprint that the Lord has for your future. Every day, work on what is true north for you today, - how is what you're working on today fulfilling what the Father wants you to do?

That warfare isn't to replace every activity in your life but it will describe to you the territory you are supposed to move into, occupy and dispossess. A lot of that battle will be right in your mind, which is why the Bible talks about the helmet of salvation and the sword of the spirit going hand in hand. With the helmet, what you are going to have to do is call down thoughts and imaginations and hold tight to the picture of what the Father showed you. The other part is going to war with every part that comes into your mind that doesn't agree with what the future looks like. 'Character' is the foundation of the height that God is taking you to. If you can expand your character triangle all the way out, to the full foundation, then the Lord can take you to the full height of what he's called you to do.

Your Strategy for Pre-eminence

Jay Abraham used the term "strategy for pre-eminence". He would talk about how you needed more than one strategy in your arsenal. I love these words from Daniel 5:12 and 6:3; the words used to describe Daniel was 'excellent spirit', the Hebrew word 'yatir' which literally means 'the mountain that has pre-eminence over all the others'. God wants you to have an excellent spirit; something that represents the connection of your character and the unique revelation of knowledge that God gave you, mixed with the supernatural, the anointing of your assignment. A strategy of pre-eminence is all about how God is going to work through you, and with you, to give you a platform where you can stand out on the mountain of your assignment.

What is it you're called to do best? Who are you called to do it for and where are they? What's the demographic that you are called to? What's the psychographic? Convergence for everyone involves a certain sphere of influence where you have a unique authority. In Joshua chapter 1 God gave a specific geographic definition on the sphere of Pre-eminence that Joshua had to stand in. Learning how to stand in the territory that God gives you is key. *"There shall not any man be able to stand before thee all the days of thy life: as I was with Moses, so I will be with thee: I will not fail thee, nor forsake thee. Be strong and of a good courage: for unto this people shalt thou divide for an inheritance the land, which I sware unto their fathers to give them."* (Joshua 1:5-6.)

3 to thrive:

What do I have to know that I don't know now? What skill will I or my team have to master that we haven't mastered yet? Who will I have to be that I've never been before?

What are the 3 things you need to have knowledge of now that you didn't have before? What are the 3 execution skills that you need now that you've never mastered before? What are the 3 areas of personal constraint where your strengths are getting in your way?

Once you identified the 3 things needed to thrive in each area, it should be obvious to you that we're going to start with the first one in each area. In each quarter of your 12-month plan, you are going to be working on your knowledge, your skill and your personality. When you're done with the first move onto the second. Clarity is power - what 3 do you need to thrive in your own strategy for pre-eminence?

Summary

If I have one concern about this manuscript, it's because transformation doesn't happen because of information, transformation happens because of the integration of information with experience.

Sometimes you may need 3 legs of stability like a tripod and 3 or 4 reference experiences of the knowledge that you are trying to tie into. For example, if you are trying to be more confident or whatever it is you are trying to achieve, you probably need 3 very strong reference experiences of doing it and pulling it off in, order to be able to update your identity. The most important part of this section is that you have to play with abandon, you have to be full tilt on this thing. It's not the information, it's the experiences you have with the information, that creates the multiplied fast track to transformation. It's the mixing of the knowledge with your own emotion and physical experience that creates a body, soul and spirit radical updating of identity. You're going to walk out of this with results that far exceed any experience you've ever had in your life, because God wants you to be able to experience life at a Level 10.

PART TWO: THE MODEL PRODUCTIVITY

With the productivity models, we will look at groundwork for optimizing in life's resources for individuals and businesses. Parkinson's Law states: 'work expands to fill the time available for its completion'; when you don't prioritize all tasks become equal and fill the same amount of time and space. However, no two tasks are equal. If you allow unimportant tasks to take priority over income-generating tasks, they will fill all the time you have and there will be no space for important and highest leverage/value tasks.

Therefore, high prioritisation of key results areas and income-generating tasks and hard procrastination of low-level tasks is essential for maximum productivity. You will also need a personal feedback and metric or measurement tool for every area with high priority in your personal and business life, including Key Result Areas, Key Performance Indicator, Income-Generating Task, Vision and Values.

High performers self-monitor more than their peers.

We will use the following model to discuss productivity: Vision, Value, KRA, IGT, KPI (V.V.K.I.K).

To access your progress and productivity, start at the top of the list of vitals below and check that you know and are doing them - then your actions will naturally be right for maximum inspiration and results. Some people start at the bottom of the list because life tells them to work harder, dig faster, and stay busy on unimportant tasks to feel productive. The higher up the V.V.K.I.K you work, the more the ones below them fall into place.

Vision: Do you have a clear picture and outcome of the purpose you want your life to serve? The contribution you want to leave? How you want to be remembered and the difference you made on the planet? Set your roadmap for your life and you'll know which direction to take, even when you hit setbacks and diversions. Regularly check back in on your vision to remove overwhelm and procrastination.

Values: the things that are most important to you in your life, unique to you, where you are an inspired genius. Are your actions in line with what is most important to you in your life? Do you even know what they are consciously, on paper? You naturally know, because this is where you naturally spend the most time, are in the state of flow, where time flies, and your results show; but if you are not conscious of them, you are not in control of them. Either make your action/focus/vocation important to you or link the short-term action to how it serves your highest values, and you will follow through with the task, no matter how easy or challenging it is in the transient moment. It also helps you know what to give up on and what to stay the distance on.

KRA's: Key Result Areas are the highest value areas you focus on to achieve your vision. These could be 3-7 areas to spend your time to make the maximum difference to your team, company and contribution. These are often strategic, leveraged operations such as developing and maintaining relationships, building an amazing team, developing systems, building a £million+ network and constant self-education. If you get stuck or dragged into micro day-to-day tasks, check them against your KRA's to remove all distractions and low-level tasks. If you have staff you must create these in your KRA or have them shifted to other people's KRA's to direct their focus too.

IGT's: Income-Generating Tasks are the highest value to you (or your company) - tasks that align with your KRA's, to maximise revenue per hour, minute and second. These are the tasks that bring the highest, leveraged results in the optimum amount of time, bringing in the maximum benefit and revenue without wastage. Overwhelm and procrastination on your to-do list can come from lack of focus on IGT's, putting equal importance on all tasks, or lacking order of IGT priority.

KPI's: Key Performance Indicators are the important, non-vanity metrics of your business that keep it moving forward, reduce mistakes and optimise leverage. They are the vital data sets that tell you in as real-time as possible exactly what is happening in your business. These become more and more vital as you grow and hand over control. The most common mistake is to delay these, so you can focus on working hard and making sales because you could be working hard in the wrong direction and selling at a loss.

You now have a cyclical feedback loop to constantly stay on track, be in flow doing the things that matter the most to you, serve the most people and manifest your unique legacy. You deserve to spend time withyourself and get some quiet time. Work from the top down and see your life take a course that makes the biggest difference. Discipline is required to keep up and build habits.

If you want more discipline that builds habits:

1. Make every day matter. I believe everyday matters because I have lost a lot of days, people I care about and opportunities. Make each day your masterpiece; if you remember how important the day is, you will not squander it anymore. Every day matters, is a growth mindset; growth can become a good addiction, a habit. When every day matters you make very different choices. When you know that at the end of your life you will ask yourself questions about how you have spent your life, you will see each day differently and also make value-based decisions for yourself and those around you. I encourage personal development for two reasons – it forces you to grow and you are empowered to help other people grow.

2. Raise your vision. The reason why lots of people are not disciplined is because they are not trying anything significant that will inspire the discipline. You have to have a big dream to pull yourself out of self-pity, slumber and the list goes on, you can't just rely on your mood to make you disciplined because that will be a dangerous place to be. Have something that pulls you which will give you the inspiration. People on the path of purpose have no time for dreamers because for them the bigger mission washes away all the silliness.

Raise your ambition to stay disciplined.

Chronos Opportunity Models

Here, we will look at some life management approaches that enhance productivity. They include – Ti Ts Tw, LI M2 DL, IGT /IGV, 80/20 IGV, RoTI, TOC and DDDD.

Ti Ts Tw: Time invented, Time spent and Time wasted

To build a foundation for the time usage, it is my understanding that time can be wasted, spent or invested.

Time invested is time that continues to earn or give leverage long after that activity is completed. Ti has residual and recurring benefits. Fresh knowledge, which you can leverage for your entire life, and that gives you better results, is Ti. Many valuable Ti activities do not always pay immediately but will pay long-term in the future or even in eternity, when followed through - like building a team, networking, building systems, leading and time with mentors. You can choose to do the things you want to and delegate and leverage the rest, so you have time to lead all that serves your vision.

Time spent is time that can bring low or high emotional or financial benefits, but little to no residual benefit. Working for an average salary or exchanging your time for money are examples of Ts because you don't get ongoing recurring value. Work you do that is not high on your value and not leading towards your vision is also Ts.

Time wasted is activities that just drain your time without adding any value or wealth benefit.

LI M2 DL

Leverage first/ Manage second/ Do last!

When you become busy, you may think 'I have got so much to do', 'where do I start' or 'when can I get this one done'?

The next time you start your to-do list or task, instead of starting with a task, start with what you can outsource or leverage. In other words, who can you get to do the first task you were going to do? If you have 6 items on your list for a day and you outsourced 3, you may have achieved double the results for half the time if the 6 tasks carry equal resource requirement.

However, when you leverage out tasks you would ordinarily do yourself, the tasks will need to be managed through to completion. An hour moved from 'doing' to 'leveraging' has enormous benefits. You can decide to have a mixture where you leverage and manage 4 tasks and do 2 tasks yourself.

IGT/IGV

In terms of business and being shrewd financially, one way to know if you are leveraging correctly is by checking that the tasks you are doing, are of the highest financial value to you and that you are outsourcing tasks below your financial value. To do this you need to start by knowing your worth per hour of your time.

The first stage is to assess your Income-Generating Value. Your IGV is what you are worth per hour of work. After you know the current value of what an hour of your time is worth, you can then assess what task you should do yourself and what task you should leverage out. To compute your IGV, sum up the number of hours you spend working every week – the total amount of time credited to earning money. This could be something like 58 hours. Then calculate how much you earn in that timeframe, excluding items like gifts and loans. If you have a monthly income, divide your figure by 4.3 to get a weekly figure. Then divide the sum of gross income by the sum of works hours and you have your IGV – your time value per hour; in other words, every hour your work brings an average of £XXX.

IGV = total income per week/hours worked per week.

For example, if your IGV is £51.72 and your hours worked per week is 56, every task that will bring in more than £51.72 per hour is OK for you to do - this can be a do task on your 'to leverage' list. You can do this task yourself without reducing your IGV, but every task that brings in less than £51.72 should be outsourced or else your IGV will go downhill. You will notice that this compounds, as when you free time from lower value tasks to higher value tasks, you generate higher value - which brings in more money and which then compounds back into your IGV. This is one reason why people don't get rich working longer employed hours or doing overtime and why the rich get richer as they leverage by outsourcing and paying for lower value tasks. You need self-discipline, to stick to this approach and for it to work long-term, as, if you keep doing tasks that will earn you higher than your IGV, then your IGV will keep going higher and higher.

80/20 IGV

When we add the 80/20 principle to the IGV or your earning capacity, we have a different picture, as it shows that 80% of your IGV comes from 20% of the things you do.

This means that you earn 4 times your IGV in $1/5^{th}$ of the time you work and you earn just $1/5^{th}$ of your money in 80% of the time you work, in terms of the real value you deliver. Spending $4/5^{th}$ of your time to earn $1/5^{th}$ of your total income is draining and does not provide financial benefits. The difference between high IGV (20%) and low IGV (80%) is much - as your high IGV 20% time earns 16 times more money than your low 80% IGV time. This difference can be changed using a work journal and paying the price of discipline. If you need to compute this:

20/80 IGV = total income per week x 0.8 /hours worked per week x 0.2

80/20 IGV = total income per week x 0.2 /hours worked per week x 0.8

Keeping a Work Journal

For a couple of weeks, create a simple work journal of how you are using your work time. You can create a work document on your phone or use a sheet of paper. You essentially need to honestly note briefly what you did, including wasted time or distracted tasks and at the end of each day put the letter IGT next to the portions that were income generating. At the end of two weeks work out the percentage of your time spent on IGTs.

When you know where you are spending your time, you can implement the 20/80 leverage for maximum financial gain with minimal effort and wastage by fo-

cusing and doing only the highest IGTs and outsourcing or giving up the rest. This approach will dramatically improve your free time and earning capacity.

RoTI

Return on time invested is a method of functioning and a model. It is a way of thinking that helps you analyse how you are using your time by consistently asking: "Will this offer the best return on time invested to me?"

This question will make you keep checking how well you are using your time and will force you to explore how to earn the maximum amount of benefit or wealth with the minimum amount of time. It will get you to leverage and create residual and passive benefit in every role.

TOC: Time opportunity cost is the cost of the current task or time spent. Some people can see the benefit or drawback of what they are doing, but not the benefit or downside of what they are not doing or could be doing. In economic terms, opportunity cost is simple to quantify.

If, for example, you have cash as a fixed deposit in the bank and the interest rate is net 2.4% compared to a net return of 5.5% on a property, then the opportunity cost is net 3.1% by leaving the money in the bank. You acquire 2.4% interest in the bank, but it costs 3.1% by not having the money in the property.

Time is less measurable to many, but the concept is the same. It's not just what you are doing that is costing or making you money, it is what you aren't doing. We need to keep monitoring and measuring how we invest our time and what we are not doing with our time.

4D: Do, Delegate, Defer or Delete is a 4-part system and personal leverage on the choices you have for any task. There are only four choices which help with confusion, overwhelm and frustration.

To-do list: Writing things down has proven beneficial; however, it's important to have a sustainable approach where we do the most important thing first. Below are some approaches that are proven.

WISDOM AND CREATIVITY

Wisdom is profitable to direct, wisdom shows you the profitable way to direct your energy and labour. With wisdom, you can anticipate what people are going to do. Every tree is known by its roots, everything that people do is a by-product of something below the surface. The root system is hidden and the fruit system is what you see. If you know what drives people's behaviour in the root, you can anticipate what they will do. Some people are even a mystery to themselves. My view is not to make it complicated, in other words, you only need to understand four emotional drivers and need types which are beneath temperament. These four are:

1. Certainty
2. Uncertainty/Variety
3. Significance
4. Connection/Love

Certainty: Assurance you can avoid pain and gain pleasure or safety or security, this is the emotional drive that you have in you, to be able to know that something will be constant. We all have a certainty need to a certain degree. If you have a high need for certainty you like to have the facts or information or the details. High-certainty people have a need to know that things are going to be the way they are told they are going to be; things need to be clear, correct, and done right; they like or need to be in control. These with high uncertainty need are driven by an entirely opposite emotional need - it is the love of chaos, the love of the unknown, it is the thrill of possibilities. When you have a high uncertainty need you have a need for variety and stimulus; therefore, you are turned on by the unknown.

Uncertainty/Variety: The need for the unknown, change, new stimuli, adventure. When you have a high certainty need you are annoyed by people like this who need uncertainty. Mega churches are built by people with high certainty needs; they tend to see prophetic people like cartoon characters because they look at the prophetic as flaky, while people that are highly intuitive find mega church structure and philosophy stifling. One represents management expertise, the MBA world of church growth which is cause and effect, metrics and predictability and the other one represents the spontaneous wind of the spirit (and by the way both are God's attributes) - you have to know which one you are. A third driver of human behaviour is called Significance.

Significance: The feeling of being unique, of value, importance or needed; in a sense it is what makes or sets you apart from others, so you are independent of the rest of the pack. Some people become significant by being the opposite of everyone else. In a family of people that are a certain way, the person that has a primary significance need will frequently behaviour the opposite way, not even because they believe what they are doing, but because they want to stand out from the crowd - they like to be popular.

Connection/Love: the connection drive is a strong feeling of closeness or union with someone or something - it is the need to become one with. The connection drive connects us with ourselves when we are emotionally alone. One of the discoveries that were made about addiction to cigarettes is that it is not always the nicotine; the nicotine is the physical addiction. The psychological addiction to smoking is that when people will take a break to smoke, you notice that they take off and their eyes kind of drifts off, because the very act of smoking is a connecting with them with their own feeling moment, a moment when they step outside and connect with their feelings, with themselves, reaching to the core. Connection is where intimacy and love comes from; if you have a person with a high connection need, they will want to be able to have a degree of emotional accessibility, time, congruence, intimacy; like the musician having a connection with the audience or the writer having a connection with the reader, it is the yearning for that connection that distinguishes one fourth of the drivers of humanity.

Out of all the drivers that drive human behaviour, uncertainty significance can drive people crazy in politics or media or the workplace because you are not working with their playbook.

The question is: Out of these 4, which one is dominant in your life, which one is secondary and tertiary? We all have a bit of all 4, but which drive drives you the most? If you have uncertainty significance, you have a Donald J. Trump (God's

Cyrus) crazy type of driver because nobody quite knows what you are capable of doing - you could do anything, you could be so unpredictable, you could function in uncertainty and yet at the end of the day your goal is to come out on top and win (significance).

Your passion is going to be connected to the meeting and fulfilment of a core human need. Some jobs don't pay well to be creative - they just want you to do the same thing all the time so you can get a certain result. Many people have a frustration trying to find the work that is fulfilling because it does not meet their need for stimulus and variety.

Growth: an expansion of capacity, capability or understanding. Growth can become an addiction - not all addictions are bad, like the addition to learning, to growth, the addiction to God's presence. Addiction can be positive or negative. The gang culture is where 4 or more of these needs are being meant in a bad way. Your yearning for growth will sanctify these 4 drives. To reach your potential you must grow, to grow you must be highly intentional about it. Growth doesn't just happen. To become a better human being, you need to grow in character. To enrich your soul, growth is needed spiritually. To be a better parent or friend, you need to grow in relationships. The specifics of growth changes from person to person, but the principles are the same for every person. The book "The 15 Invaluable Laws of Growth" by John C. Maxwell, will help you understand the growth gap between you and your dream and potential.

Contribution: a sense of service and focus on helping, giving to and supporting others. Growth and contribution sanitize the human four drivers. Any strength over-extended becomes a weakness.

Your success in life will be based on knowing who you are, what God calls you to do, being able to manage who you are in what God called you to do, in various sessions of doing the assignment. People will always rationalise their decisions based on their human need unless, it is sanctified by a commitment to growth and contribution, which makes you objective, and hear what God is saying.

Wisdom and creativity are related. The Hebrew word for Wisdom is 'hochma', one of the meanings of 'hochma' is *creative skill*. It's what gives a craftsman the ability to take raw materials and turn them into objects of beauty. Wisdom is the ability to take the raw materials of life your and skilfully turn it into something of beauty. Creativity is a manifestation of wisdom in the context of excellence and integrity. Wisdom is personified in Proverbs 8 and is the companion of God at the creation of all things. Wisdom and creativity must not be separated in the mind. They are essential tools needed to complete our assignment and in being an effective witness to the lost. It is wisdom that makes your role desirable.

Creativity that illustrates the presence of wisdom.

> *"When He set for the sea its boundary; So that the water would not transgress His command; When He marked out the foundations of the earth; Then I was beside Him, as a master workman; And I was daily His delight, rejoicing always before Him, rejoicing in the world, His earth, and having my delight in the sons of men."* (Proverbs 8:29-31)

While most people have a value of wisdom, most do not have an equal value for the role of creativity in their God-given responsibilities. Yet it is creativity that illustrates the presence of wisdom: *"Wisdom is vindicated by all her children"* (Luke 7:35 NASB). The six days of recreation saw the most wonderful display of wisdom and art imaginable. As God spoke, the worlds were made. Light and beauty, sound and colour, all flowed together seamlessly as wisdom set the boundaries for creation itself. Solomon, the man known for supernatural wisdom, discusses the co-labouring effect that wisdom had on that day in Proverbs 8. One purpose of wisdom is to show us difference and distinction. Wisdom is also the study of difference: Difference in people, difference in environment, difference in our countenance, difference in an opportunity.

Wisdom is given an artisan title of "master workman." Note the even more powerful phrases; *"rejoicing always before Him," "rejoicing in the world,"* and *"my delight in the sons of men."* Wisdom is not stoic as it is so often pictured. It's even more than happy; it is celebratory in nature and finds pleasure in the act of creation. But its greatest delight is in us! It has found perfect companionship with humanity. We were born to partner with wisdom – to live in it and display it through creative expression.

Do you sometimes think you need wise counsel to make decisions in your business? Ask God! He is ready to help. You may need to hire consultants, coaches or a mentor for some roles. My experience is that God is the best counsel giver for the joined-up view.

> *"Then Pharaoh said to Joseph, "Since [your] God has shown you all this, there is no one as discerning and clear-headed and wise as you are.You shall have charge over my house, and all my people shall be governed according to your word and pay respect [to you with reverence, submission, and obedience]; only in [matters of] the throne will I be greater than you [in Egypt]."* (Genesis 41:39-40)

No matter how bad things got, Joseph always trusted God as the source of wisdom. But no matter where he was thrown, or what was thrown at him, Joseph turned to God for wisdom to make decisions. He ended up running the household of his master, then running the prison and in the end, running the foreign nation that had taken him captive – Egypt!

Pure and True Wisdom

We are all invited to share in the wisdom of God. Christ and His Cross are the foundation of the power and wisdom of God. From the most brilliant scholar to the poorest of the poor uneducated child in the bush of Africa, whoever calls on His name shall be saved. It is simple enough for a child, and yet its depths are greater than any of us can ever fathom. To the human pride, it is offensive, because it values something that we can never do for ourselves. But God has revealed His wisdom to us in His Son, and we can choose to embrace His Cross and share its good news wherever we go. According to the Bible, denying the Cross is unwise thinking. There is the wisdom of this world, and then there is God-thinking. It doesn't matter how many degrees you have without Christ, the epicentre of the glory of God will be missing because the conclusions you draw are going to be missing the revelation of the power and wisdom of God that comes through Jesus and the Cross.

LEVERAGE

BUSINESS LEVERAGE

The number one factor to scale your business quickly is leverage because there's only so much time. You need leverage, so it's not all dependent upon you. There are two important kinds of leverage. There are systems and people. Though you need finance to acquire systems and people, having the finance is just part of the beginning. You can use systems to automate your processes or to maximise your exposure to various channels like online or you can hire and lead people. The reality is any great business needs to be able to do both. Some business owners freak out or get very unsure when it comes to hiring and leading people because they either don't know how to do it or they've had a really bad experience doing it. We will focus more on people in this section and deal with systems in a later chapter.

Hiring and Leading People

Deal Flow: There are two reasons that can make hiring people hard. The first is no deal flow. They come up with a poor job advert and they post it someplace and they get just three responses, so they invite them all to an interview and one of them doesn't show up. The other one shows up drunk, so they end up giving it by default to the least inferior option and then they wonder why they've got problems with their people. You need deal flow. Deal flow is having a high selection, an array of options to make the best choice from. If you only see three potential candidates, you're going to end up with the best out of the three. Whereas if you've screened or you've had 20 or 30 or 50 or 100 different CVs of people that have applied for the position and then you interview the top dozen or 20, then you take the best five or six and get them back for a second interview. Your chances of success increase exponentially.

No Target: The second reason why people don't succeed when it comes to hiring and leading people is they've not defined success. I don't like most job descriptions much. The reason why I dislike them is they're nebulous. They don't actually tell you enough. Let's say you're hiring for a marketing position and you go, "Okay, so I'm looking for a marketing executive who can get advertisements on social media and then distribute them to our sales team." Really that's all the adverts say - all the people that got experience.

They know how to advertise their product the best way and get good quality leads, but they don't quantify what any of that means. When they get somebody in, as long as that person's seemingly doing the tasks called, appraising the advertisements and getting some leads then, they're deemed to have been doing an acceptable job. There's no way of measuring of whether it's an acceptable job, a good job, a great job, or an exceptional job.

Instead of job descriptions, I prefer job scorecards. This concept/approach will change your business. Rather than saying, "Okay, these are the activities that the person needs to do," quantify what success looks like. In this marketing executive example, you say you've got to get leads. Well, how many leads? You might say, success looks like getting in excess of 1,000 leads per month. But that's not all.

You might say, "Well, certainly I can get you 1,000 leads, but they're all really useless leads." You say, "Well, the second criterion is that those leads convert to paying customers, at a rate in excess of 11%." But then it's possible that somebody can get you a high volume of leads that convert, but they spent so much to do it you can't make any profit.

The third criteria might be that the cost has to be less than £2 a lead. Therefore, you've defined what success looks like. It looks like a marketing executive that's getting leads on social media in excess of 1,000 leads a month at less than £2 per lead and those leads must convert to a rate greater than 11%. In other words, it's going to give you more than 110 customers. Now you know what success looks like, so if you're hiring somebody at £25,000 a year or £35,000 or on a £50,000 a year salary, you can quantify what would equal a good return on investment. At the end of the day, a business activity is spending money to either get customers or keep the customers that they've got.

Any expenditure the business makes is an investment. You need to quantify what is success, what is an acceptable return on investment, to know whether or not it's working. If you do that, your chances of getting good people and leading good people and getting great results increase exponentially.

A great question is, how do you motivate and get the best out of your team? Well, I believe people come to work wanting to succeed. Nobody comes in going, "Oh, I really want to do a substandard, minimal job today." They want to succeed, but some employers haven't set up the game so that the employees can win - because they haven't given them the scorecard. They haven't given them the three key metrics. That's what I recommend. I don't recommend more. I really don't recommend less. Three key metrics are so you can quantify and measure success in that job role.

My experience is people want to excel if you show them what success looks like. If you ever had to fire somebody or had a bad experience, the worst firing is where the person didn't see it coming because you thought they were doing a bad job, but they thought they were doing a good job. It will be a misalignment of expectations. You need to clarify the situation by giving them the metrics, but how do you drive the accountability? I believe that the performance metrics should be done company-wide.

It is a good idea to have a team-wide meeting where people sit down, once a week or once in two weeks, and they share their three metrics. Specifically, they forecast what they're going to do next week and then when it gets to next week, they update it with the actual performance that they had. If I am using the marketing executive as an example, the number of leads generated, the cost per lead, the conversion rate of those leads, etc., but then they also forecast the next week and everybody is aware. Doing this activity company-wide makes everybody aware of what everybody else is doing.

It facilitates conversations and questions to be asked. Since if somebody is not performing, I'd rather everybody knew about it sooner. Why? Because it may not be their fault. It may be because they're not getting the resource or support need, or they're just overworked, or it's unrealistic targets, or they just may be underperforming. The point is that facilitating an open conversation creates a culture of accountability and drives better performance.

My experience of managing teams of employees comes down to a few simple principles. Don't micromanage. Look, demand the best and very often you'll get it, but you need to call it tight. What does that mean? The best way to get an A player to underperform is to put them in a team of B and C players. You get what you tolerate and if you tolerate people slacking off and underperforming, then you're going to create a culture of underperformance.

Some business owners aren't prepared to have the tough conversations. They're not prepared to say it as it is, but the reality is that if you've defined what success looks like and you're having the conversations regularly (via a company weekly meeting), it's easier to drive better performers. You nip it in the bud. Kill the monster while it's small. Don't make it this big dramatic problem where it feels awkward.

When you manage people, you should be calling it tight when they slip up, touching base with them, letting them know that you're aware of it and seeing how you can support them - knowing that you believe they can do the job because that's why you hired them in the first place. What can you do to help? One, you identify the cause of the non-performance and you go right ahead and address it. If you're calling it tight by consistently supporting your team and expecting and demanding high performance, very often you'll get it.

In my journey, I have seen people with inferior performance, that needed to be fired by their company, being tolerated, with senior management was wondering why they were struggling in the unit, and their profits obviously down. The unit lead was showing up as a manager, not a leader. However, the senior executives had also not properly defined what success meant. They'd not called it tight and this created a culture of mainly B and C players, where even the A players or the better performers were underperforming.

My experience has been to get the best from your team, you need to create a culture of honour; however, you still need to call it tight and that very often that means you should hire slow and fire fast. Easy to say, of course, but not as easy to do; but if you've defined success and you're incrementally calling it tight ... the unsuitable players will, very often, leave if they're not performing and you'll get a much higher level of performance from your team.

At the end of the day, if you want world-class performance and a world-class culture, you've got to have fun. You've got to enjoy being together. Gazelle companies are growing fast, which means that the people within them have to grow fast.

If your company's not growing, it's because your people aren't growing.

How can you inspire them? How can you support them more? If they feel supported, they will crawl over broken glass to get the results for your company. That's the culture that you want.

Richard Branson has a great quote. He says, "You want to train your people, so they can go and get any job in the marketplace, but treat them so well that they won't want to." That, I feel, is the definition of a great culture.

PERSONAL LEVERAGE

Personal leverage is about leveraging life. It is about how to set your life up as an employee or entrepreneur or business owner by getting more done in less time, outsourcing everything except what you have to do and love to do, and setting up and scaling your lifestyle. To scale you will need a personal design with elements of the followings building blocks; strategy, systems, concept and tactics.

Leveraging Money

You can start by working hard for your money on a job and then gradually transition to your money working hard for you. This transition requires growth and a paradigm shift. You can be a slave to money, or money can be a servant to you. You can exchange time for money, or you can build assets that create fairly passive income that preserves your time. If you don't have any of these assets listed below under assets working for you, you will be working for your money. You will be spending your time preserving it rather than investing or leveraging it.

One way to create income and capital, and still preserve time, is through assets. You invest time and capital (where relevant/necessary) in assets that produce (passive) income. You set them up, get them managed by people or systems, then you exclude yourself from the operation of them.

In an economic sense, an investment is the purchase of goods that are not consumed today but are used in the future, to create wealth. In finance, an investment is a monetary asset purchased with the idea that the asset will provide income in the future or appreciate and be sold at a higher price.

There are some levels of using money. We have to first move up the ranks, knowing how to spend, save, invest, speculate, insure and give. The more knowledge you acquire at each level, the more money you will make and the greatest your impact. Giving should actually start at the saving level; however, you can't give or save what you don't have.

Leverage Assets

There are some assets which form the building blocks for other assets. See them as the foundational or primary assets:

1. Contacts (Relationships);

2. Knowledge/Skill; (IP, tested ideas/patents/licences/information/music/software ...);

3. Time;

4. Money (Finance);

5. Health.

When you combine these foundational asset areas, and you leverage other people in these areas, the results you are looking for will come faster and without you having to be chief cook and bottle washer for everything.

The next type of assets we can classify as secondary assets because you need the primary assets to maintain and multiply them. This list is by no way exhaustive:

• A business (physical or e-Commerce);

• Investments (stocks, bonds, paper, etc.);

- Money lending;

- Partnerships (franchise, joint ventures, etc.);

- Physical (precious metals, art, watches, wine, classic cars);

- Property;

- Your Brand.

When you start investing, you should look for relatively low-risk investments with a relatively low knowledge barrier. Stocks, property and a business venture you have knowledge in are probably the lowest barriers from a standing start, as the risks are low compared to more volatile or speculative alternatives if invested properly.

Leveraging People and Skills

Leveraging people and skills simply means, leveraging the skills of other people. When you went to primary and secondary school, you had a teacher that understood the subjects better than you. It's a cultural norm that it's OK to leave your kids for a larger proportion of their waking day in the trustworthy hands of the teachers. When you got your 30m badge, you learned from someone who could swim well. When you took your driving lessons, you used a qualified instructor. When you go to the doctors you put trust and faith in their skill and prescriptions. You trust you'll get the correct diagnosis and dosage of a treatment that could cause you harm if taken in excess.

Some people don't have the same faith, attitude and behaviour in business and life. They ridicule 'self-help' and they say, 'Why do people have life coaches, trainers, relationship advice, business coaches and money mentors to help create their ideal life?', and while for them in the most important things and areas in life they are feeling their way in the dark, having to make all the blunders, slips and mistakes themselves without counsel, support, collaboration and accountability. Most wealthy and successful people invest continually and intentionally in coaches, mentors and in their network.

Bill Gates has frequently been listed as the richest person in the world. Gates credits part of his success to his mentor, businessman and investor, Warren Buffett. During an interview with CBC, Gates credited Buffett for teaching him how to deal with tough situations and how to think long-term. Gates also greatly admires Buffett's desire to teach things that are complex and put them in a simple form, so that people can understand and get the benefit of all his experience. The first step to finding a great mentor is admitting you can benefit from a mentor – 'Understandably there's a lot of ego, nervous energy and parental pride involved, especially with one or two-person start-ups. Going it alone is an admirable, but foolhardy and highly-flawed approach to taking on the world' (Richard Branson).

Simon Cowell, the producer of the highly successful TV shows, X-Factor, America's Got Talent and more has discussed turning to a mentor, billionaire British Businessman Sir Phillip Green, after feeling overwhelmed by life. In a candid interview with The Guardian, Cowell disclosed that he had experienced difficulty in coping. "I was trying to deal with everything — my business, the artists, the shows, everything," he said.

Leveraging the knowledge and skills of other people, particularly those more experienced than you in your field is, without a doubt, one of the best ways to improve your skills quickly and efficiently, leading you on the road to wealth faster than if you were to learn by trial and error on your own. All the greats had mentors. Learn from the best if you want to be the best.

LEARNING

Conversation is the seed for every desire we have. Every change of season comes out of a conversation and conversations are the birthplace of miracles. A question controls your information and knowledge. Until you ask a question, other people control your knowledge. A question is one of the quickest ways into your future as a question is a powerful force on the earth. Your advancement in life will happen at the speed of your questions, the right questions. A question is the proof of humility. Humility is a proof of something you don't know, a recognition of something you don't have. God reacts to learners.

I seek to become a world-class learner. The Bible is a book full of questions. One moment that God gave us is a picture of Jesus at the age of 12. He was asking questions of the leaders, and when his mother rushed up to him, he asked her a question. "Must I not be about my Father's business?" Jesus loved questions so much he answered questions with a question. Questions are doors, questions reveal passion, questions reveal interest, and questions reveal humility. In Acts 16, the Philippian jailer could not even come to Christ until he asked the question of Paul, "What must I do to be saved?" A question opens your life to knowledge. Nothing is more powerful than a question.

Time does not guarantee change, applied knowledge does. I don't normally look for answers for anything, I look for the right question. I know that if I can ask the right question, the answer is the employee of the question. My questions host answers on the earth. You should continuously ask yourself questions. What could I do that would simplify my life in 24 hours? What task should I assign to others? Your future depends on what you're willing to ignore. Your comfort is determined by who you're willing to train. Questions like "What am I willing to live without?", "If I knew I had 12 days left to live, what would I do differently?" "In whose presence am I energized for my assignment?", "If I were to die tonight, whose prayers would matter to me the most?" "Who are the two people that trust me more than anyone else?", "If I could be alone on an island, and could have one person with me, who would it be and why?". There are many, many, many questions to ask. I believe with all of my heart that when you begin to ask yourself questions, wrong things will fall off of your life.

I want to remind you that it's possible that you've never asked yourself the right questions.

A question is the proof of passion and desire.

Wisdom and Creativity help us to see that everything has a different value, every relationship has a different reward, and every season has different fruits. Personal questions that can change your life include, "whose counsel do you pursue with passion?". I cannot change your life till I change the voice you trust. A key difference in seasons is the voice you trust. The difference in success and failure is the voice of a mentor. The changes I go through in life are proportionate to my applied knowledge. God is a teacher and he is looking for protégés. Questions come to us all the time; one key is to ask the dumb questions until you get to the smart ones - don't try to qualify them. You obviously can't learn everything; to succeed, you need to know what you want; what you want to express, change. You have got to have questions to confirm what you know. Ask questions relentlessly.

Learning Entities

A learning organization is an organization skilled at two things: creating, acquiring, interpreting, transferring, and retaining knowledge, and second, acting - modifying its behaviour to respond to the new knowledge and insights. Unpacking this definition from Professor David Garvin, first, a knowledge or learning organization works with ideas. It comes up with new ideas, moves them throughout the organization, and somehow keeps them whole in policies, processes or reviews. And second, it actually acts. It takes the new knowledge as a basis for responding to a changing environment.

This suggests the three building blocks:

- The learning processes, which the definition really emphasizes;
- The learning environment that makes those processes possible;
- The leadership that really fosters and inspires the learning processes and helps create the learning environment.

Why is it so important for individuals and companies to be learning entities? To satisfy this question, we will use a telling quotation from Ray Stata. Stata was for many years CEO of Analog Devices, a semiconductor company. And he said, "the rate at which organizations and individuals learn may well become the only sustainable competitive advantage." Products can be copied and services can be copied. Processes can be copied and things like Six Sigma are available on the open market. But if you're learning more rapidly than the competition, you can get ahead and stay ahead. Also, the world is changing - we have a more global environment. Industry boundaries are collapsing and previously regulated businesses are becoming deregulated. We've got new business models. If your rate of learning isn't greater than that rate of change, you're going to fall behind.

We've shown the value of being a learning organization. Why is it so difficult to be one? What are some of the hurdles companies need to overcome? Let us look at three reasons:

First, some of the early discussions of the learning organization were abstract and without concrete prescriptions for action.

Second, the concept was really aimed at the CEO or other members of C-level executives, rather than at the local leaders who are leading focused work projects, departments, divisions, business units in the organization itself, where the critical work of the organization is done. Where they can think about 'what do I need to do tomorrow to help my organization learn more readily'?

And third, there was a real lack of standards or tools with which managers could assess how well their organization was doing in being a learning organization.

All three of those barriers need to be addressed to make the concept more actionable and more accessible. One company that meets the test of being a learning organization is GE. In Jack Welch's last letter to shareholders in their annual report, he said, "I finally realized why we're so successful. It's because we're a learning organization." They have the processes, they have the climate, and clearly, they have the leadership behaviours.

There are a number of things that managers can do to help their teams contribute to the company's learning. One, for example, is to help their teams have a supportive learning environment. For instance, we think about the concept of psychological safety, where people perceive that the local social environment is one that is comfortable for asking questions, admitting mistakes, floating wild ideas, and just taking those kinds of interpersonal risks that are absolutely essential to learning. Culture can't be taken for granted in most organizations; however, managers can do a lot to improve the culture for their teams. Another example: the chief operating officer can institute a policy like "blame-free reporting" to allow people at all levels throughout the organization to speak up with their observation of mistakes, anything they thought might not be going well, and be free from penalty or blame.

In some sense, what this implies is visibly going out of their way to help people be comfortable with the very real risks that exist in the workplace today so that they can engage in the learning processes described. This may sound almost as if it's being nice or just being tolerant, but it's actually not about being nice. On the one hand, it's about respecting other people. But it's really about being tough-minded enough to brutally confront the facts, to talk directly about what works and what doesn't work. It's about being straightforward. It's not about being overly friendly, but about being open. And, I think, about respecting each other enough to be willing to engage in that kind of openness.

Some of the concrete practices companies can put in place include:

- A supportive learning environment, a climate that tolerates mistakes and errors.
- Concrete processes and procedures; forms for experimentation, forms for sharing knowledge and best practices; ways of reflecting on what employees have learned from past experiences. Each of these are processes and systematic steps – step by step by step – where companies generate ideas, respond to new knowledge, and reflect on what they've already learned.

This does not have to be bureaucratic. In fact, some of the most powerful learning processes are also the simplest. Take the US Army. They have a process called after-action reviews. It's a post-thought. It's a reflection on what we've learned from our experience, our mission, our project, our activity. It's organized around four simple questions:

1. What did we set out to do? What was our objective, what were we trying to accomplish?
2. What actually happened? It sets up the facts, the actual details of what went on.
3. Why was there a difference? Often there's a gap between our objective and the reality.
4. What do we do next time? What activities do we sustain or continue, and what activities do we improve or do differently?

That's not at all bureaucratic. It's simply a systematic way of going about reflecting on past practice. If you are a manager and have bought into this concept and you understand the need to be a learning organization, but you don't see your organization as a whole really encouraging this in a systematic way, you can still make this happen for your team. You can. In fact, that's the right place to start even if you could influence the whole organization. What you need to do, as a manager working within the organization is start with your group. And start simply by modelling the behaviours yourself. Show curiosity. Ask a lot of questions. Admit when things are puzzling or not going right. Acknowledge the uncertainty that's out there and invite others' input. It sounds so simple, but this is the leadership that creates the environment in which these more structured processes can take form.

PRODUCT CREATION

The product creation process starts with evaluating and updating the customer problem identified, followed by a product vision.

Describe Your Idea

To start the process of designing a well-crafted and effective value proposition, consider the following aspects of your business idea. Be honest and answer as completely as possible.

1. Who is your target customer? What kind of problem do you solve for them?

2. Is this an important problem for this customer? Is it an urgent problem?

3. How do you plan to solve this problem for the customer? Describe how your solution will work in the customer's hands and the benefits that it will generate.

4. Who is your competition? How do they solve this problem for their customers today?

5. What is unique about your way of solving the problem? Why are you better than anyone else in solving this problem? Is your advantage sustainable over time?

"A product's value proposition is a statement of the functional, emotional and self-expressive benefits delivered by the brand that provide value to the target customer."

This definition consists of several key components:

A.   What you offer to customers;
B.   What type of value or benefit is associated with your offering and how much of it the customer can expect, as well as how the value is generated;

C.   To whom you are offering that value.

The key point to note at this stage is that value proposition concerns the most fundamental aspects of a new venture. We will focus on which decisions entrepreneurs should make to inform the value proposition and how to get those decisions right.

Informing this section are the principles of customer development and the "Lean" movement as professed by Steve Blank, Eric Ries and Ash Maurya. As stated in Blank: "A start-up is an idea searching for a business model." The entrepreneur and the start-up team are investigators who, through their roles in the start-up, seek answers to gain a level of certainty that did not exist at the outset. Through a process of experimenting, learning and iterating, the entrepreneur can (and should) test the key assumptions underpinning the business. The uncomfortable outcome of this learning process is that entrepreneurs might discover that some of the initial assumptions underpinning their business idea are not true - and cause them to either change or abandon the idea altogether.

This is a good thing. Keep in mind that the purpose of the Lean philosophy is to avoid "waste," and the thinking is that the learning process will ultimately help you to glean a viable idea whether you are bootstrapping or building a venture-capital funded business. This might differ from the idea you started with, but you will end up with a more sustainable venture.

In the first two steps of the three-step process, we focus on the value proposition. The first step involves problem discovery and the second step validates your proposed solution - both key parts of your value proposition. In the third step, we use the validated value proposition to create a sustainable business model for the new venture.

Things you like to do should be a hobby of yours, but things the world does should be a business of yours - Warren Buffet.

The decisions to identify your target customer, what problem you will solve for that customer and which features your solution should have (the key decisions that inform your value proposition) must be made before you begin designing your business model. Why? Because the decisions that concern your business model depend on your value proposition.

For example, you cannot determine what channels to use for customer acquisition, communication and distribution if you do not know your target customer. You also cannot decide what kind of relationship to have with those customers or how to charge them, since the basis for payment is tightly connected to the problem being solved and the characteristics of your solution to the problem. If you do not make the decisions concerning the value proposition before delving into the business model, then you risk becoming mired in a decision process that is not properly anchored and has no measurable end.

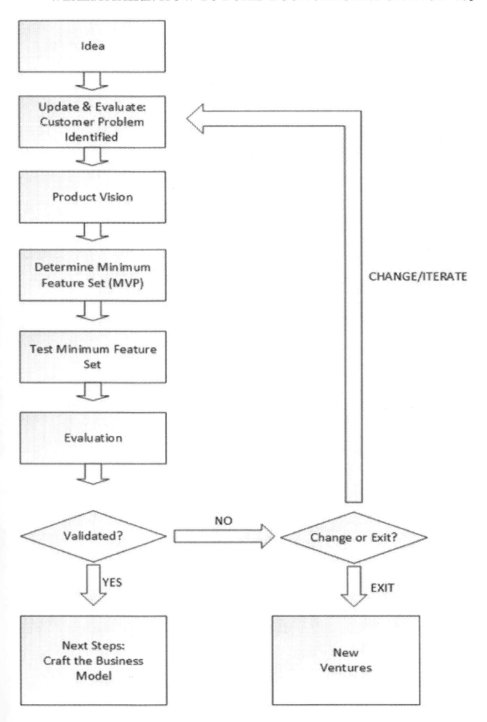

Value Proposition Process

Crystallize Your Value Proposition Assumptions

This activity builds on the "Describe your idea" activity and helps you to examine the basis for each answer you provide about your target customer and the problem you will solve for them:

> 1. Is the customer problem you are solving validated by a measurable fact?

> 2. Are you able to identify which customers are suffering the most from this problem?

> 3. Do you understand how the problem impacts the customer and their business?

> 4. Do you have evidence that links the customer problem to the target customer?

For each answer to the questions above, determine why you believe this answer is true. Do you have solid, objective evidence in the form of measurable facts or have you made an assumption that you believe to be true?

1. In the cases where you have facts, label the answer as "Fact" and list the evidence. The evidence could be primary or secondary research, a series of observations made by you and your team, or a systematic problem reported by potential customers and industry insiders.

2. In the cases where you have made an assumption, label the answer as "Assumption."

Complete the activity by listing all the assumptions you have made regarding the customer problem and the target customer. The next section will address how to test those assumptions.

Testing Your Target Customer Assumptions

A customer need or want arises when a customer has a problem that he or she feels must be addressed. It follows then that when entrepreneurs create a value proposition, they need to focus on what customer problems exist in their field. The entrepreneur's objective is to gain a detailed understanding of the nature of those problems. This begs the question, "How do you know when a customer has a problem?"

The presence of a problem tends to be more obvious in the world of business than in the consumer market. Most people in business pursue concrete and measurable objectives related to revenue, profits, cost, production and market share. A failure to meet those objectives often constitutes both an organizational and a personal problem.

On the other hand, in the consumer world, the objectives pursued are highly diverse and often more difficult to measure. Other than the obvious objectives driven by our need to eat, drink, sleep and be safe, consumers pursue a wide range of functional, social and emotional objectives - a meaningful career, a healthy body, great relationships, a cleaner environment, a safe family, a solid education and so forth

Test Your Target Customer Assumptions

If your idea is currently based on untested assumptions, you must seek to validate those assumptions. In this section, please describe how you plan to obtain the evidence. Determine how to best validate the assumptions. For each assumption assess:

   1. What key piece of information would validate or invalidate the assumption?

   2. Where does that information reside?

   3. What is the best way to gather that information?

Make a plan to carry out this validation activity. It might be helpful to consider what market research techniques are available to you.

Ensure that you test your assumptions so that you can answer the following questions with confidence:

a. What objectives are your potential target customers pursuing?

b. How are they pursuing the objectives?

c. How does failure to reach those objectives affect them?

d. Can the impact be measured in economic terms as a loss?

Whether we are considering businesses or individuals, a problem arises when a person recognizes that they are failing to reach an objective. The realization that your current situation is not what you desire causes *cognitive dissonance* - a sense of mental conflict, slight irritation or even anger about the situation being imperfect. Cognitive dissonance lies at the core of a customer problem: it triggers the motivation to find a solution. Advertising and other sales or marketing initiatives are designed to cause cognitive dissonance by suggesting to the customer that life is better with the advertised product than without it.

However, most entrepreneurs face a situation where people are generally unaware of their new product and are therefore unable to consider how life would be different with their new product. When your target customers do not recognize that their situations have the potential to be different, they experience no cognitive dissonance and thus no perceived problem. In such a situation, your customers have a *latent problem*. For most entrepreneurs with innovative products, the presence of a latent problem signals that their marketing must begin by discrediting the status quo, which is the current way of doing things. They need to show how current solutions are failing in the areas that they can address with their new solution or technology.

However, when crafting a value proposition, it is important to understand that most target customers cannot be expected to explicitly know or understand the presence of latent problems for the reasons just explained. The focus of investigation must therefore involve understanding their "jobs to be done" (i.e., what they are trying to achieve) and what challenges they face in getting those jobs done. In other words, what stands in the way of the target customer being satisfied with their situation?

Conducting Customer Interviews

1. Start your interviews with people you know;
2. Remember to position the interview as a non-sales conversation (your purpose is not to sell);
3. Be well versed on key trends in your industry and what your interviewee and their organization are doing;
4. Ask open ended-questions;
5. When the interview is over, systematically document the information gathered. In most cases, the interviewee will be happy to answer any follow-up questions;
6. Be respectful of everyone's time and demonstrate proper meeting etiquette. Turn off your mobile phone during the meeting and follow up with a timely thank-you email. If the interviewee provided referrals and introductions to other candidates, then follow up to let them know the outcome of those introductions.

Evaluate Market Feedback

1. Is the market problem urgent?

2. Is the market problem pervasive?

3. Will your buyers pay to have this problem solved?

If you answered "Yes" to all of the preceding questions, then you will have identified a problem that is worth solving. The biggest source of waste in any start-up is building something that nobody wants.

I've lived the experience of building things that people didn't want, and eventually finding out how to build something that people actually want. "One way that you actually build something that people love is by building incrementally." The lean start-up advocates an iterative approach to building a business or product, with each iteration teaching you something actionable. As every start-up is unique, it is impossible to account for every variation of a problem a venture might encounter. The entrepreneur and start-up team will need to make many key decisions to best fit their situation. Nevertheless, it is key to strike a balance between being prescriptive where there are best practices to employ while maintaining the flexibility to allow start-ups to act on their individual opportunities and circumstances.

Deciding on Your First Customers

It might seem like an odd idea to "decide" who your first customers should be. After all, most customers decide to become your customers by themselves; it is not your decision to make. However, through the process of validating the customer problem, you will have learned a tremendous amount about the marketplace and about individual customers and their needs. Based on that knowledge, you should be able to identify what your first target customers should look like.

Create Your Initial Target List

1. For B2B (business-to-business) scenarios: Examine your contacts and the conversations you have had with them. Create a list of target economic and technical buyers that fit the criteria mentioned earlier in this product creation section.

2. For B2C (business-to-consumer) scenarios: Examine your contacts and the conversations you have had with them.

Product Vision

The product vision is a description of how you imagine your idea as a fully developed product in the hands of the customer. The concept of the whole product might be helpful in terms of formulating the product vision. At this stage, there are two key reasons to document your vision:

1. Internal: Initially, your vision is the target of your product development efforts. In other words, a description of the vision is critical to ensure that your team and partners are on the same page.

2. External: Your first customers to buy products based on the potential rather than actual state. It is fully possible that you can land an order from a visionary based on a well-documented product vision and an 80% finished solution. In other words, a well-documented product vision is your most important sales tool in the early stages.

Create a Day-in-the-life Scenario

Use a day-in-the-life scenario to help gain insight into what your product should be doing/does for the target customer. The day-in-the-life scenario is similar to television shows in the "makeover" genre (e.g., Extreme Home Makeover) in that it describes a "before" situation where the customer does not have your product and then an "after' situation where the customer has your product. The "before" situation is covered by the first four questions below; the "after" situation is covered by the last three questions. Complete a day-in-the-life scenario by answering the following questions:

1. Who is the target customer? Personify your target customer: give them a name, an age, a gender and a job description. Imagine them as real people with real problems.

2. What is their objective? What are they trying to do?

3. What challenges are they facing in pursuing those objectives and what is the economic impact of not achieving those objectives?

4. Imagine the customer using your product. What are your product's qualities or capabilities?

5. In what way do those capabilities affect the customer's ability to achieve those objectives?

6. What is the measurable benefit of achieving those objectives?

It is important to address each question in a day-in-the–life scenario with as much accuracy as possible, especially the third, fifth and sixth points. In the end, the day-in-the–life scenario helps to pinpoint how your product changes the situation for the customer and the impact of that change.

Describe Your Product Vision

There are many ways to describe a product. In general, a product vision should be short on technical detail and rich in customer-relevant descriptions. You can create your product vision by writing brief responses to the points below as a typical product vision should cover the following topics:

1. Your target customers and their problem;

2. The product solution you are making;

3. How the user goes about their job and will use the product solution;

4. Customer outcomes and benefits;

5. Three- and five-year scenarios for your product and company.

Testing the Product Solution: The Minimum Viable Product

For this phase of your planning efforts, it is important to remember that potential customers are rarely capable of discussing desirable features for products they have not seen or experienced. It is up to you to find a way to translate your information into a desirable feature set. There can be expected talk about the desirable qualities of a process that they already know and the outcomes of that process. The *Minimum Viable Product (MVP)* is generally defined as the smallest number of features that your first customers are willing to pay for (either directly with money or indirectly by spending their time using your product).

However, in his book *Lean Start-up* (2011), Eric Ries offers a slight variation on the definition: "The MVP is the minimum set of features required to learn from early evangelists." This definition is very useful in our context, since the MVP's primary goal at this stage is to expose it to potential customers and get their feedback on a number of critical business assumptions rather than induce an actual transaction. In line with the philosophy of customer development, the purpose of the MVP is to avoid spending time, money and other resources on developing features that customers are unwilling to pay for. Avoiding this type of waste will result in shorter product development timelines and a faster avenue to sales revenue.

Create the MVP

The MVP can be many things. However, since the purpose of the MVP is to learn through customer feedback, look for the most efficient way to help customers imagine having and using the product. MVPs range from slide decks to more functioning products or a combination of the following items as examples:

- Slide deck or images or brochure or animated movie or video

- Non-functioning prototype or functioning prototype or beta version (software/web)

- "Light" version of product

Whatever format your MVP takes, make sure that the MVP is an effective way of getting feedback on your product idea. In this world of Internet-based media, applications and tablet/smartphone apps, the process of changing your solution's features and iterating new solutions for further testing can be done both quickly and cost effectively. The advent of ever-improved 3D printing is creating similar opportunities for many physical products, although with larger product solutions the concept of iteration is naturally restricted to reviewing blueprints and possibly models made to scale.

Test the MVP

In general, testing the product idea involves presenting your MVP to potential customers and possibly having them use the product. As with testing the customer problem, make sure to inform users that you are not trying to sell something to them, as you are simply interested in their feedback. However, it is likely that your first customers will emerge from the group that you subject to the testing - a positive side-effect of the time you spend learning about and improving your business. As you engage with potential customers in this round of testing, you want their feedback on both functional and non-functional issues. Specific questions to which you want answers include:

1. Is our understanding of the customer problem accurate and relevant?

2. Does the MVP solve the customer's problem?

3. Does the product solve the problem better than a viable alternative currently on the market?

4. Would they use the product? Can they imagine the product as part of their everyday life?

5. What is their primary concern about buying and implementing the product?

6. How much would they be willing to pay for the product?

7. What process would the customer employ when deciding to buy such a product?

8. Who is involved in the decision-making process?

9. Whose budget will the funding come from?

10. Who will be the users of the product?

Summary:

1. Test the meaningful problem/solution.
2. Who is your ideal customer and are there enough of them?
3. Explore Crowdsourcing your product/service and create a V.1 MVP (Minimum Viable Product) as soon as possible & iterate from there?
4. Can you monetise it?
5. Test your product/service/IP with low overhead, low risk, first and

    fast.

6. Get feedback and iterate.
7. Pivot frequently and don't be too attached to what you want; Rolls Royce/Coca-Cola each started as other business models and evolved.
8. Repeat this process for each product/service you launch, and check in yearly that your existing business is still doing this.
9. Do you have or need an IP, license, patent, trademark or none of the above?

BUSINESS MODEL CREATION

The purpose of this section is to capture the process of developing a comprehensive business model.

"A business model describes the value an organization offers its customers and illustrates the capabilities and resources required to create, market and deliver this value and to generate profitable, sustainable revenue streams." (Osterwalder, A., Pigneur, Y., & Tucci, C. (May 2005). Clarifying Business Models: Origins, Present and Future of the Concept. Communications of the Association for Information Systems, Volume 15). This definition is particularly useful for entrepreneurs because it is based on a holistic perspective of the business and emphasizes the sustainability aspect of a business model.

Parts of this section draw on the work of Alex Osterwalder and Yves Pigneur, who provided the definition of a business model. Entrepreneurs who are in the process of designing their business model require an approach that allows them to understand if and how a value proposition can be successfully scaled up to a profitable business. Today's business is threatened by all kind of things; consequently, businesses need to constantly evolve to meet the wants of the customer. Every business at one point will have their business model challenged. The moment you have an opportunity to present a concept that the customer wants, someone is going to fill that void; hence challenging the existing models and value proposition.

Key Business Model Questions

To begin the process of designing the business model, please answer the following questions. Answer as accurately as possible because you will need this information later in the process.

> 1. How do you acquire customers? Briefly describe the steps involved, the amount of time required, the typical value of a deal and the stakeholders required (including the people on your side and the customers' side) to sign a new deal.

2. After you have landed a new customer, how do you plan to relate to that customer and manage the relationship (if at all)?

3. How do you charge your customers? What is your revenue model?

4. How much do you charge your customers? Can you calculate your revenues for the next month, quarter and year?

5. What assets are available to you or under your control?

6. Who are your key partners?

7. What key activities do you need to engage in to deliver your value proposition?

8. What are your fixed costs?

9. What are your variable costs? Can you calculate your total cost for the next month, quarter and year?

10. Does your revenue forecast demonstrate increased profitability toward the end of the forecast period?

Based on our definition of a business model, it is clear that many factors must be factored in when designing a business model, which makes it a more complex task. Therefore, we recommend that entrepreneurs use the Operations Business Model Canvas (OBMC, a visual tool created by Alexander Osterwalder) to facilitate the design process. The visual component of the tool simplifies the design process by making it easier to understand how the various components of a business affect each other. It also enables you to involve the rest of your team and advisors in the process.

The OBMC consists of nine interrelated building blocks, which are briefly described below in the order each block is typically addressed. Once you become more familiar with the contents of each building block and the flow between the related blocks, the OBMC will become easier to use. The OBMC is versatile, as it can be used to design a business model.

Customer segments: This building block involves describing the target customer.

Channels: When addressing this building block, you must determine how to connect the value proposition with the target customer. The term "channels" refers to three different facets of making connections - communication, sales and logistics.

Customer relationships: What type of customer relationship do your customers expect to have with you? The nature of the relationship can follow directly from your value proposition.

Revenue streams: Revenue stream is not the same as price, although these terms are related in the sense that what and how you charge your customers impacts your revenue stream. At a basic level, your revenue streams define your business model. For innovative products that produce a new and unique value for customers, you might need to innovate with respect to what and how to charge. When deciding your revenue model, it is also important to develop a fundamental understanding of how your customers make money to ensure that your revenue model is not at odds with your customers' business needs.

Key resources: The first building block on the left side of the Business Model Canvas requires you to consider the resources needed to create your value proposition. In this context, resources mean any relevant intellectual property (IP), technical expertise, human resources, financial and physical assets, key contracts and relationships. In other words, resources refer to anything within your control that can be leveraged to create and market your value proposition.

Key partners: For a new venture in the early stages, the purpose of a partnership is to ensure that you have a product offering that appeals to your target market. In other words, the partnership complements your resources and key activities as required to deliver your value proposition.

Key activities: This building block describes the key processes that are required to weave together your resources with those offered by your partners to deliver the value proposition, manage channels and relationships, and generate revenue

Cost structure: This building block examines the cost of delivering the value proposition, including the resources needed and key activities involved. We want to answer the following key question: does the cost structure provide a reasonable profit?

Create Your Own Business Model

Describe your operational business model by completing the Business Model Canvas.

1. Use the value proposition you crafted in the product creation activities section as your starting point.

2. Use the answers from "Key business model questions" to help you complete the rest of the OBMC.

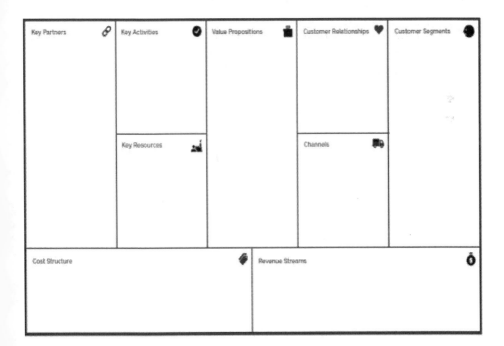

Operations Business Model Canvas

Consider Your Business Model

Having completed the canvas, it is time to step back and consider it in its entirety:

1. Does it work? Do the revenues outweigh the costs?

2. What are the risks to your business model? What parts of your business model are most critical for your business to grow in a profitable manner?

3. Are there things that can or should be changed to strengthen the business model or reduce its risk?

I recommend working through these questions with your team and/or your advisors to ensure that you develop a shared understanding of the key characteristics of the business model.

Clarify Your Business Model Assumptions

The first step in the process is to clarify the key assumptions that underpin your business model. Building on your completed OBMC, we will examine the basis for each building block of your business model.

Check each response in the Operations Building Model Canvas against the following

criteria: How do you know what you wrote in each building block is true? Have you made an assumption or do you have solid evidence - in the form of documented facts? In the cases you have facts, label the response as "Fact" and make a note of your evidence. In the cases you have made assumptions, label the response as "Assumption."

Complete the activity by listing all the assumptions regarding your business model. The next activity is testing those assumptions.

Testing Your Business Model Assumptions

Here we will seek to validate the key assumptions underpinning your business model. However, some assumptions about your business model are more important than others, so we should prioritize and focus on a few key assumptions rather than test all of them. Steve Blank's customer validation process is based on the premise that a business requires a *repeatable sales process* to grow successfully. For a new venture facing customer scarcity, Blank's assertion is valid – without a repeatable sales process, that business will have difficulty finding growth, attracting investors and building economical processes. However, not all businesses face customer scarcity, for example:

1. If the business is involved with property or infrastructure development, the main bottleneck is often in de-risking the project to the point where it is financeable. De-risking a project can be time-consuming and requires a robust understanding of the project's regulatory environment hurdles as well as funding.

2. In some businesses, access to expertise and talent might be a bigger obstacle to growth than finding customers. For instance, in the pharmaceutical (or other regulated) industry, the expertise required to traverse and influence regulatory requirements can be more fundamental to the sustainability of your business model than a repeatable sales process.

3. When we look at the commodity business, the strongest bottlenecks normally include, securing access to the resource and extracting its profitability, and not finding customers.

However, for the purposes of this section, we will assume that your venture is neither heavily regulated nor in the resource space. The obstacle standing between you and business growth is the ability to acquire new customers in a repeatable manner. For such a venture, you should focus on testing your channel, customer relationship and revenue stream assumptions.

Blank's method for testing those assumptions is simple: Get in front of potential customers and try to sell your product solution! At this stage, it is important to know that a few deals will provide sufficient validation - until you see a pattern emerge with respect to the sales process: length, deal size, final deliverable, services, etc. Blank's approach rests on the notion that real customer insight can only be extracted once you put them in a situation that might involve handing over money and/or time.

1. By closing a few deals, you will uncover the customers' concerns with your company and your product, as well as the steps involved in overcoming those concerns.

2. Going through the sales cycle (lead, prospect, qualified prospect, committed and transacted) several times will help you to identify and understand the key buyers typically involved in evaluating and signing off on the deal.

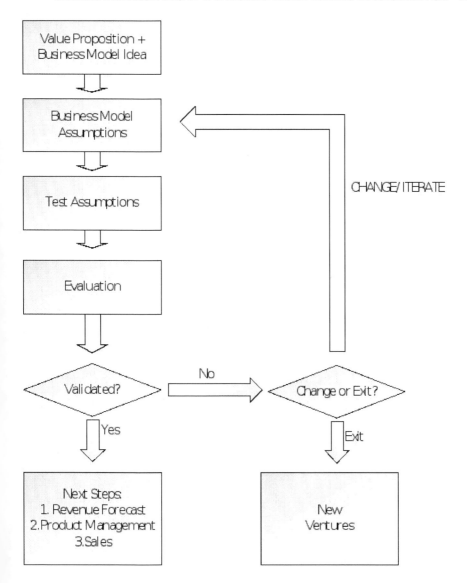

Business Model Process

After testing your business model assumptions, depending on the complexity of your product solution, landing your first few deals might take time. It is important to not lose focus on the overarching objective of this process, which is to validate your model and sales process. Systematically review the experience of selling to customers by evaluating and updating your documentation.

Next steps: Having completed your OBMC, you are ready to implement your business model.

To complement the OBMC use "The Business Model Navigator: 55 Models That Will Revolutionise Your Business" by Oliver Gassmann and Karolin Franken Berger. The Business Model Navigator is highly informative; its content provides practical insights on how to innovate business models and may be of particular interest to managers engaged in the organizational creativity journey and educators delivering modules on entrepreneurship and technology commercialization. The text highlights the potential value of creative business models for enterprise and presents a structured approach for how managers can effectively design novel business models specific to their organizational context.

The core value of the book lies in the authors defining of 55 patterns of business model and real-life examples that both educates the reader as to the scope/diversity of business model design and how they can develop models for their own enterprise through 'creative imitation and recombination'. The thorough and comprehensive research of the authors in defining these 55 patterns provides the reader with the cognitive 'building blocks' to unlock their creative potential and build unique business models to add value to their enterprise.

Paradigm for Model Creation

I heard a coach say, "When it comes to enterprise, you should do what you love." I believe this is a myth for most business setups, as my view in a sense is the enterprise is not the vehicle to fulfil my "dreams", the enterprise is the vehicle through which I fulfil the dreams of the consumer(s) and they, in turn, reward me for my service. The rewards provide the opportunities for me to pursue my vision. The birth place of enterprise is demand. Don't become like Nokia - they lived their dreams but forgot to wake up! Demand is the baby that never stops crying and in today's age you can feed it the same thing but it can't know it. *Today's success is not just 'in demand' but is also 'on-demand'!* The new 'on-demand phenomenon means that you able to meet what the consumer want swiftly. Take iPhone for instance, who manage each time to convince us that we are getting something different and we are willing each time to swallow the proverbial broccoli hiding nice and tidy.

Detailed business plans are not good for early-stage ideas: Elaborate business plans for early ideas points at one of the biggest hurdles to innovation in large corporations. Business plans inflate the risk of failure of your business idea and encourage teams to refine an untested concept/idea. Move away from detailed business plans for early-stage ideas. Although the intention behind senior executive requesting a business plan is benevolent, it will often do more harm than good to a nascent business idea. Business plans are great documents for executing on a known and validated idea, but they're not very useful if you're just starting to search, design, and test new value propositions and business models.

It's a common routine inside companies: individuals and teams have a flood of great ideas that can create value for customers and the business where leadership's first reaction is to pick an idea and instruct people to develop a detailed business plan. The habit of writing detailed business plans for untested ideas can cause big failures, leadership needs to understand the value of testing and validating underlying assumptions of all early-stage concepts, to unearth hidden details. However, any idea must have a first cut business plan or there is no compass for the value it provides - if you can't articulate the need, the unique insight and approach, and the competitive landscape - what are you talking about?

Trust experiments over experts: A detailed business plan assumes you know all the answers for a given idea. That's hardly the case. Teams spend hours compiling fantastic forecasts and will spend lots of money, hiring people to build technology or products that have no evidence to support their success. You can always make the numbers look good in a plan and argue how well it will work, but the plan will mean absolutely nothing without rigorous testing and evidence. Companies like FLO TV (under Qualcomm) and Better Place (a provider of battery switching stations for electric cars) both failed because of great plans full of assumptions, opinions and forecasts that never turned out to be true.

Both companies started building expensive infrastructure and technology well before understanding if the assumptions around their value propositions and business models would work. Those were some pretty expensive failures, and they didn't have to be. The learning is Better Place managed to raise and squander $850 million because the company assumed its plan would work. Untested business plans rarely have enough evidence to support the plan. In cultural terms, leaders and teams have to value evidence over opinion. A small experiment can generate clear evidence to validate or invalidate an idea, which then warrants further learning and testing before deciding if something is worth scaling.

Understand that innovation isn't expensive: There's this myth that big company innovation has to be expensive, and we know that's just not true. Innovation is really a series of calculated investments in a portfolio of experiments. Rather than placing all of your resources and budget into one big "wild gamble", leaders should be encouraged to test many ideas cheaply, and gradually increase investment as more evidence is gathered. Managers should embrace very quick and cheap experimentation. This will allow teams to gather evidence and validate or invalidate assumptions. The process of agile and nimble testing will reduce risk because teams will learn faster, and iterate ideas, based on the knowledge gathered. You'll also go to market quicker with a better sense of what your customers really want.

Understand that profitability matters: Start-ups that used to enjoy raised capital are now anxious to become profitable. Companies such as Birch box, Dropbox and Jawbone have started cutting back on costs as external financing has become scarcer. Why? There are countless companies that ran out of money before they could build a business model that's profitable and scalable. Although 'product-market fit' is key to succeeding, don't forget that a great value proposition won't save your company if your business model isn't sustainable.

You could be leaving money on the table (or dissuading customers) if you set your prices based on what competitors price, or based on how much margin you want to make. If your value proposition is differentiated, consider pricing it based on how much value you deliver to customers. Why: Once again, it comes down to understanding what people want, care about, and how much value (not features!) you provide. Customers are generally happy to pay for something when they get their problem solved.

SYSTEMS

A business can be sectioned into 5 key parts: Sales, Marketing, Finance, Delivery (operation) and People. A system helps run your business by integrating all the five parts of a business listed above. A system breaks down your businesses processes and sets verifiable checkpoints with expected outcomes for each task. A system will provide services, a service has both Data and Logic and it takes action based on information received. One service usually handles one business object or function and designed to achieve a specific result. For example, Fleet is a service that manages a collection of vehicles. Most business owners fail to put systems in at the right time and break as a result. For a small company, a comprehensive system is much more than a simple how-to document; it's more like an organic collaboration of ideas and validations, constantly updated by every member of the team to find the minimal number of steps necessary to maximize return on investment.

The system needs replicable processes that can be automated or delegated and which allows you the option of removing yourself from the business. As the business grows the system(s) should begin to cater for strategy and creativity, the customer decision journey, process automation, organization, technology, and data and analytics. Setting up a system is easier said than done, and no system is a one-size-fits-all.

For a start-up, one of the ways to scale, systemise and leverage, is to get a part-time personal assistant or virtual assistant and task them to hold you to account, and you sending them everything you do on a daily basis in note or video or audio. As you can use the PA or VA to create your initial systems and manuals, so you can do less of what you have assigned to them, make more and focus on growing your enterprise. They collate, type and organise everything you send them, getting your PA/VA to do it gives you accountability, like having a Person Trainer. Getting a PA/VA to help with a system is an important element so when you are preparing for hiring or sale - it may take longer than planned and disrupt existing business functions.

Start this process now of getting you OUT of your business, and in turn, give your PA/VA work.

For a start-up the following steps can be used to start creating a system:

1. Make a note of what you do as you do it in headings or sub-headings and transfer it to a mind map.

2. Send it to a virtual or personal assistant to type up and order your manuals with clear page refs and indexes, and send back to you within an agreed time-frame to check.

3. Record anything you say on an App or Dictaphone (sales, marketing, scripts, processes, right down to how to log in) and send the audio file to your PA/VA. (Use dictation function on phone; you can even do it via email on iPhone using the 'mic' icon)

4. Read the manual(s) once a month as if you know nothing about the role; ask, could anyone step in and do this role following this manual? Then feed-back tweaks to your VA, ensuring they keep it organised with clear contents and page no. refs.

5. Then as you grow and scale you instruct your various team members to do the same, where managers manage down, and your PA can be responsible for yours.

For micro and small businesses, the following steps can be used to continue creating the system:

1. Take an inventory and identify what actions you take regularly that help drive your business and let go of having to do everything.

2. Using business case, use cases and requirements and take a snapshot of where the going needs to go and make room for discovery-driven growth.

3. Prepare thorough step-by-step manuals for current use cases and requirements.

4. Create processes and brainstorm ways this process can become either a) automated or b) most efficient.

5. Implement.

6. Hire employees you can trust to build a team.

7. Continuously improve and create a two-way training process.

8. Track each system's efficiency.

9. Leave room for error, and expect it.

Most start-up entrepreneurs want to be hands-on every step of the way, but this is a common growth limiter. Making your business successful means letting go of control over every detail and making employees accountable for doing their jobs. When you implement simple systems for your most essential business processes like cleaning, ordering, etc., you can step away knowing that most of these systems will go according to plan. You can confidently delegate repetitive tasks to employees which can't be automated, yet freeing yourself to work on areas of the business that generate additional cash flow. Any processes that you can't fully automate should be batched, including some social media campaigns, monthly ordering, and more.

A good process will include training materials, which may be how-to procedures, templates, worksheets, sample orders, bills, or other documents, spreadsheets, a workflow chart or software, an FAQ page, and any other information needed to perform the task at hand. Checklists are especially handy to ensure consistency and quality. Each task can be broken into steps and checked off when complete. A simple, shared document portal can help in the delegation process. For complex situations, implement an open-ended decision process that helps you test assumptions and use cases and use line-of-sight decision-making. Line-of-sight decision-making is where you, as a business owner or team lead, realize that no system will cover every possible scenario, so you trust your team to solve most problems they will encounter. Let your team decide the best medium for solving the problem. In real life, most problems aren't as simple, but it illustrates why hiring and effectively managing A-list players is important.

Most successful systems should also have a simple feedback loop built in. This feedback loop will make it easy to see when things are going as planned and when they aren't. Reviewing feedback can be as simple as a weekly or monthly check with team members or as complex as financial modelling based on performance data. As the business grows, these feedback loops will allow the system to become more and more focused. In a business, sometimes often, things don't go according to plan, so your systems need to be flexible enough to account for that. These unexpected events are a great time for you to trust in yourself and your team to figure things out what went wrong and fix it in your system so you don't make the same mistakes again. If I asked you, "What do you do on a daily, weekly, monthly basis that helps create and run your business area?", then you might come back with 4 or 5 core elements – the things you create in your business area, along with the things you do to actually help it run as a business. Each of your systems requires that a certain number of steps be taken in order for it to work, and those steps come together to make up a process. For example, your marketing system is made up of a lot of smaller pieces – actions and events that you take in order for "marketing" to actually exist within your business. This actually presents systems within a system and we see that marketing also has systems within it, like social media, advertising, partnerships, sponsorships, and so on.

BUSINESS FINANCE

Several years ago, in one of my businesses in Lagos, I was constantly pushing to grow, grow, grow, and I wrongly believed that getting more sales was the solution to all my business problems. At the end of each month, cash flow was still tight. It was a big effort meeting payroll, and I felt constantly like I was trying to push a boulder up a hill. Then I learned some things that began to change everything. I learned how to read the business scoreboard - this was before I went to Bradford business school for an MBA. If you can't read the scoreboard, you don't know the score, and if you don't know the score, you can't tell the winners from the losers. Warren Buffet said that, and it's true.

Thinking about it, if you're watching a sporting competition, would you have any interest whatsoever if the players were just running around, and nobody was keeping score, and you had no idea who was winning and who was losing? Of course not, and yet this is how most small business owners play the game. The facts are that if you want to stay in business, and you want to be profitable, you have to know how to read the scoreboard. You need good, strong management accounts. They are the feedback tool as to whether your plan's working. The numbers, the financials for your business are the effect - they tell you what activities took place in your business, and they tell you where and how you should change your strategic plan.

These are the three scorecards that you need to know at any time in the day of your business:

- Statement of profit and loss.
- Balance sheet;
- Cash flow statement.

Statement of Profit and Loss

The statement of profit and loss is the one that most business owners are familiar with.

192

The statement of profit and loss tells you three things. It tells you your sales at the top, your expenses, and then your profit or your loss. That's it. Most business owners understand this, and yet most business owners don't have great clarity on it. They wait until the end of the year and hope that the accounts give them the right numbers. In fact, a lot of people don't know how profitable they are. They know what their sales figure is, because they've seen the invoices, or they've seen the money come in, but they don't know how profitable they are. This makes zero sense. So this is the first scorecard you must understand.

Balance Sheet

A balance sheet, fundamentally speaking, tells you the net worth of your business. It tells you three key component parts. The first are assets. Assets, what are assets? Things like cash, things like stock, things like building, plans, equipment. Stuff that has a value. An asset is also an economic resource that puts money in your pocket, a liability is something that takes money out. The second section is liabilities, i.e., the stuff that you owe. It can be accounts payable (stuff that you owe to trade creditors), it can be a bank loan, it can be an overdraft facility, it can be other kinds of debts, and mortgage on a property.

The final section is owner's equity - this will tell you whether you own your assets. The left side of a balance sheet must equal the right side. You've got assets, thing and stuff that you have, and then do you have debt in order to buy that or do you own it outright?

An easy and personal example I can give you is to think of a house. If you own a property that's worth £100,000, and you've got a £75,000 mortgage on it, that would be a liability, a debt that you owe on that house. That would leave you with equity of £25,000 in that house.

So think of your profit and loss statement, also sometimes known as your 'P & L' or income statements, as your income, and then think of your balance sheet as your net worth. These two scorecards are very different documents. It's possible to have a high income but low net worth, and vice versa, so you need to understand both to be in business and to really thrive and prosper.

Cash Flow Statement

The third scorecard, which you must understand, is called the statement of cash flow and it's got three component parts. The statement of cash flow tells you how the cash moves in and out of your business, when cash comes in and when it comes out, in three areas. The first is O, for operating cash. This is money that comes in and out directly related to the operations of your business. Primarily, it's money that's coming in from sales, or its money that's going out on expenses.

The second is investing cash. 'I' is for investing cash. In other words, this is money that goes out because you're buying assets; for example, you're buying stock, or you're buying a building, or you're buying new equipment, or it comes in because you sold some of those assets.

The final one is F, for financing cash - this is money that's borrowed or repaid. When you borrow money from a bank, or you repay that money to the bank or lender to pay off that loan.

At a high level, with the three types of cash, one is substantially more critical than the others, and that's operating cash. The reason why operating cash is the most important is most business owners fail to understand that profit and cash are not the same things. In fact, have you ever heard of a business, or do you know of a business, that went out of business despite it being very profitable? Of course. It happens all the time. Seemingly fantastic businesses can go bust overnight because they don't understand these numbers. They don't understand how mistakes and screw-ups in any of these three scorecards can ruin the business. They're the three scorecards that you need to dive much deeper into to understand them, to help your business prosper.

STRATEGY

Strategy is a plan designed to achieve an overall aim. It is a plan for obtaining a specific major result.

As an individual, you need at least two concurrent strategies...

- One building wealth.
- The other building CASH FLOW!

You can use one business or more businesses to do both cash flow and wealth or use your vocation for short-term cash flow while building your long-term strategy for wealth.

Before we look at strategy, we need to decide:

- What is your WHY (you need three compelling reasons)?
- What is your Big Overall Aim (Vision)?

We need to focus on our 'why' as we go through the contradictions and process events. If you want to build the RIGHT business, one that you are proud of and love to be in and a business that you can exit (whether that means selling it on, or just being able to take time out, knowing that your infrastructure is in place) this requires strategy, which really is the core to making all of this work. But before you build your strategy, please figure out your 'why'. Because without purpose, it is all irrelevant. Strategy is not tactics. Tactics are a plan (action) for a desired end result. Tactics are like three blind men trying to describe an elephant!

"Strategy without tactics is the slowest route to victory. Tactics without Strategy is the noise before defeat" - Sun Tzu

The strategy business model canvas (SBMC) below is a great way to capture your present state and future vision and can be used as a canvas to capture the strategy conversation.

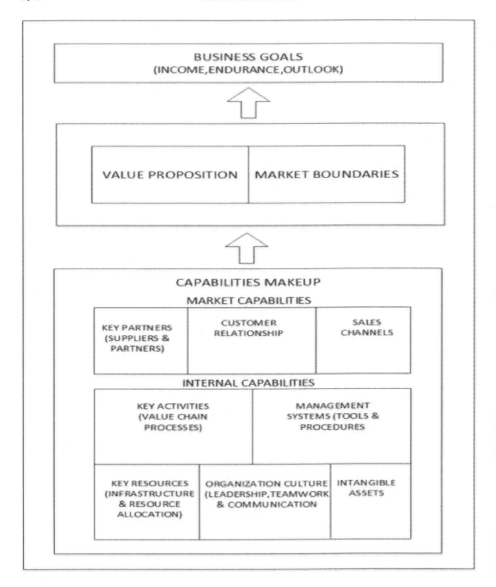

Strategy Business Model Canvas

The strategy business model canvas above is a great way to anticipate the synergy required for growth and give you a joined-up view of the south-to-north flow of activities while you do a north-to-south flow in your thinking. Don't allow your assumptions to become facts in your own mind for your core business, where you think you have a lot of predictability. A common mistake is thinking about *growth businesses* using the same mental models that are used to think about *operating businesses*. The strategy journey is about learning, about discovery, and about finding a business model that works and evolves. It is a mistake to begin it thinking you know what the linear, measurable path will be.

The future of strategy and creativity will be incredibly dynamic. Leadership and companies will have to prepare for a world where businesses will constantly have to reinvent themselves. How can you prepare for this transformation? There are three activities that leaders and teams can regularly perform to become dynamic strategic thinkers.

Companies need to prepare for a world where business models and value propositions will change regularly and dramatically. Leadership can discuss and capture where the company is now, and where the company needs to be, using these three activities, that can be regularly conducted to evaluate strategic progress.

Strategic Thinking

1. Start by looking at what you have got.

You will want to assess what the company is working on that's part of today's business. What projects or areas of the organization can be a candidate that could fuel the next generation of growth? And what are you currently working on that are potential options for the future? Are there existing resources or assets that have been overlooked, but could be repositioned to create new value for customers or the company?

2. Discuss where you want to be.

When you look out five or ten years, what are some of the things the organization wants to achieve? Where are you hoping to aim the company? From there you can work backwards and assess how it will apply to what the company is doing.

3. Then break it all down into day-to-day activities.

This is where all areas of the organization will get involved, and it's how your strategy can be implemented. You will have to translate your longer-term strategy into day-to-day activities that will consist of experiments, learning, and iterations. These tasks will all move you toward validating or invalidating the future value your company hopes to create. You will be continually gathering evidence for the organization's vision, and regularly need to assess how these new ideas or opportunities can get the company where it wants to be.

Strategic Competence

Strategic competence is the desired state or quality of a company's service or product that sustains its competitive advantage. Competence can also be applied to the improvement or development of one's abilities and skills for the benefit of the person and the group or institution that he or she represents. Competence can result in an increased quality of product or performance or service.

Competence starts from a company's capabilities. In a sense, competence is the proven abilities and improved capabilities. Competence can include a combination of processes, tools and systems, combined skill, wisdom, revelation knowledge, behaviour and organization. Strategic competence is used to fulfilled potential products. (Potential product: the apparent growth path of the benefits demonstrated by the product as it is improved, and as it is complemented and strengthened by other products and services).

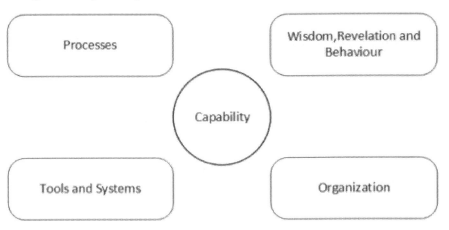

Concerning the figure above, the processes are all the things you do in order to make any given system work most efficiently. A system can be viewed as a collection of processes, in a similar area of focus. A tool is an instrument for special functions in software and system design; it has predefined inputs and delivers predefined outputs and is built for human factorized usability only. Tools are used to build frameworks. A framework is a wider term that makes room for mental creativity; it is a combination of different tools, design patterns or procedures and protocols created in order to create a wider product and services. For example, a framework can be used to create a new software system (from analysing of the necessary business cases, use cases and requirements to testing of all evaluated software modules).

The Pattern

Concerning the picture below, resources required for the production of goods and services can be generally classified into major groups: land, labour, capital and enterprise; however, these factors of production are changing and evolving with industry boundaries collapsing and a more global environment and the level of uncertainty in our time. For example, if you want to run an online trading course, your land is the Internet. These resources for production are also categorized as management, machines, material, money and knowledge, as knowledge used within a knowledge economy has come to be recognized as a distinct form of labour and a factor of production in its own right.

When you want to perform an internal audit, which you would do as part of your strategic planning, as part of your SWOT analysis (an internal audit would reveal strengths and weaknesses in your business), you want to be able to distinguish your resources from your capabilities, and then understand those capabilities, which are competencies or distinctive capabilities. One way to think about this is, the resources are what you have, capabilities are what you can do with them, and competencies are those things that you do really, really well that put you ahead of your competition.

Resources first start as inputs, the processes and people intermix with the inputs in order to create activities that can generate value for your customers, when that value is difficult to imitate, you have a competitive edge. Resources include human resources, intangibles like brands, structural or cultural inputs, the culture of your company, how motivated and driven your people are. What does a competency or a distinctive capability look like? The distinctive capability really needs to be something that allows your company to step ahead, to shine. Resources, capabilities and competencies are elements that need to be aligned for companies to have a solid foundation for deciding about which markets they're going to serve, what products and services they're going to launch, where they will grow, what acquisition targets will allow them the best leverage or enhance their capabilities, where their cost and investment should be focused, how best to organize the company around what it's great at, and so on.

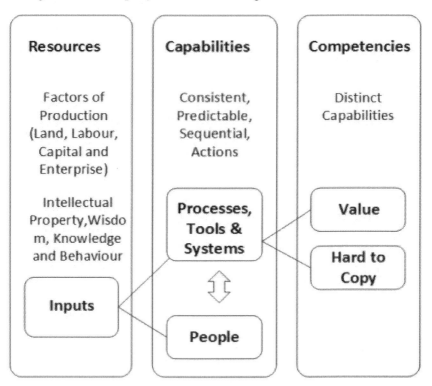

Value is created through what a company does, its capabilities, rather than what it has or sells. When you identify what you are great at and how this greatness matches with market needs, do you have a value creating strategy. A recent survey of companies in the USA showed that two out of three companies admit that they don't have the capabilities needed to create value in the marketplace. In the survey a vast majority of companies were chasing too many opportunities and most of their strategy work is done to solve specific problems. How should we grow? How can we improve a given business? What inorganic options do we have? Rarely does it ask the more fundamental questions about the company's identity, it's unique and differentiating way of creating value.

We can define a company's identity through what it does, its capabilities, rather than what it has or sells. Great products and services come and go, but great capabilities can outlast markets. Strategy therefore, must address this fundamental question: What is the company going to be great at? What are the very few capabilities that together bring the type of differentiation required by the market? These are usually no more than three to six capabilities that reinforce one another, what can be called the Differentiating Capabilities System. Successful companies know how to connect their entire business to their capabilities system. They have a clear way of creating value that the market wants, and that their capability system supports. They have a portfolio of products and services that similarly connects with their unique strengths. We can call companies that get all of this right, coherent. Strategic competence take advantage of distinct capabilities to improve and consolidate current competitive advantage, while closing the strategic coherence gaps between our existing capabilities and those required to support our strategic choices.

The Strategy Journey

The journey will require going from business idea or module (a new market, improvement to business unit, a new technology, new product or service etc.) to a profitable and scalable business model with the minimum amount of time and money wasted. Success will require deeply understanding any new market you want to enter, and a differentiated value proposition, with 'customer wants' embedded in a business model that can scale and generate profits. Also crucial to this is the right timing, in the right business environment, with the right aligned team that can assure sound execution.

LEADERSHIP

Leadership is responsibility in disguise; leadership translates to everything we do. Leadership is a lifestyle of continuous self-development, improvement and transformation. A Level 1 leader will attract Level 1 and 2 people. Leaders do not use the phrase, "I don't know". Leaders go the way and show the way - effective leaders are like tour guides, not travel agents.

John Maxwell's book "The 21 Irrefutable Laws of Leadership" details keys characteristics of leadership which will show areas we are strong in and areas we need to develop. Leaders know how to choose good mentors in areas they struggle with.

To develop in areas where you are weak, surround yourself with people good in that area or develop that area. Great leadership is timeless. Demands on leaders change from one era to another, but all great leaders possess some familiar and ageless qualities that endure across generations. We need to be leaders of leaders, not leaders of followers.

The greatest leader challenge we all have is leading ourselves.

Managing yourself well gives you integrity;

Knowing you gives you confidence;

Your vision gives you followers;

Believing your story gives you authority.

Enemies that can impact your leadership include:

- Regret of the past;
- Fear of the future;
- Shame in the present.

We need to live in the present, the now. Managing yourself has to do with everything you are as a person - to begin to know who you are, look at who is around you, the people you draw to your life. Birds of the same feather flock together. If you hang around people that talk great things and never do them you are hanging around "Pigeons" - they talk about great things and never do, and they have wings but can't fly. If you hang around people that say I want to do this, but I am afraid, then you are hanging around chickens. I want to do this but I am a bit afraid - "Chickens".

If you hang around people who keep stealing your ideas and vision, like a bird that kicks other bird's eggs out of their nest and instead of hatching its own eggs, it lets the other hatch it, you are hanging around "Cuckoos". If your friends are all show but little content you are hanging around "Peacocks" - they are flamboyant, wear beautiful suits, they look great, body manicured and pedicured; however, character is content, not the container. Looking good is great, being good is more important.

Leadership is about effectiveness, as you develop your leadership you develop your effectiveness. If you are always with dead people you are hanging around "*Vultures*", people going nowhere. The African proverb "only a stubborn fly follows the corpses to the grave", is counsel to the wise - if he is going nowhere and you choose to follow him, you are like him. There is a level you fly at where you rarely see other birds. When you see a bird you know it is an eagle - the eagle loves opposition. When there is an opposing wind, the opposing wind is the opportunity for the eagle to get higher out, to get to higher heights than any other bird.

We are destined to mount up with wings like eagles.

Modelling is the most important level of leadership, as everything stems from modelling. Leadership is first modelling, modelling makes you an example; before you can train a person you need to be the example. People do what you do not say - the first me of leadership that every leader must know is modelling.

Great leadership raises people to be their best self; people do what they see their leaders do. Jesus is a good example of a leader. He told his disciples, "the works that I do shall you do also; and greater works than these shall you do; because I go unto my Father."

The process of modelling an example to create a legacy is:

- I do, you watch;
- I do it with you;
- You do, I watch,
- You do, and let somebody watch you;

The second level is motivation. You can't lead people you can't motivate. Modelling deals with character, motivation deals with charisma. Charisma is also a gift, an anointing, an ability to use the gift that God has given you to inspire others to take action, not to be like you. A poor leader raises leaders like themselves, great leaders inspire people to be themselves, their best self. Motivation leads to encouragement. I love when people come into their uniqueness. Who are you? What is unique about you?

People need to look at our life and be inspired - lead from the front. It is not our playing small that saves the world, when we allow our light to shine, only then do we empower others.

It is not our playing small that serves the world, our playing small, our false humility, but as we allow our light to shine we sub-consciously give other the right to do so.

The next level is mentorship. Success without successors is 'failure'. If you can't replicate yourself, you are not a leader. Lone rangers always deal in addition; leaders deal in multiplication. God has commanded us to "be fruitful and multiply" - only leaders can multiply, followers can't. Mentorship leads to 'establishment'. If you want to see people around you established, you need to find them the right mentor and you your protégé.

Your mentor is not the ceiling; the mentor is the foundation. You need to go up more than they have ever been. People who train people. Mentorship is sitting down to train the next generation, become a teacher because as you teach you learn more. When the Holy Spirit is there it grows, called to raise discipline. One of the strongest ways to learn is teaching. Everybody is a teaching learner; you don't want to be the lid on your people. Mentorship establishes people. A mentor is there so you don't make major mistakes; the Holy Spirit is the greatest mentor. The higher you climb the higher you influence; the leader is the influencer and may not the person that holds the top position.

Mobilization is for empowerment - launch the people. After you launch the company, your mission is impossible - it is too big if you had what God had planned for you.

Leadership Attributes	Manifestation
Modelling	Example
Motivation	Encouragement
Mentorship	Establishment
Mobilization	Empowerment
Mastery	Ever Lasting Legacy

Questions leaders ask:

- How did I do today? How can I do better tomorrow?
- Who am I in this season?
- What is unique about me in this season?

Wisdom Key:

1. What I have done you will do greater, you have untapped potential;
2. Everybody is a teaching learner; you learn as you each.

Here's a secret. If you realise that God wants to give you all things, providing you have the capacity to handle it, and the thing that sanctifies your ability to handle anything is the ultimate affection you're serving through your success, then the real antidote to getting corrupted by premature or too much success is to have a heart completely captivated by the kingdom so that everything you've got is towards that end.

Every now and then, you can walk away from it. Give extravagantly, release your attachment to things below and prove that you are not addicted to or controlled by the success God gives you. That's a different kind of species. The "Level 10 leader".

The Level 10 leader can acquire mastery, pre-eminence, success and prestige, but not be controlled by it because they guard the nuclear core of a greater affection. Their heart is more devoted to God's kingdom and the king than the thing. They can walk away. Not easily. If it was easy, it would have no value.

Things leaders need to do regularly:

- Vision/Vision Mapping
- Speaking
- Building Teams
- Meeting the need of the team member

Leading from the Future

This is called leading from the future back. Most people are stuck in the present dreaming. Prophetically we should already have a premonition/portent of where Heaven is calling us to go, and you know what it looks like. One way to find out what the premonition of the future is that when you hear it, it excites you.

Some people are stuck on a merry-go-round "year in year out", hoping each year will be different. Our lives will remain the same except we do something. Learn something different and meet someone different because they know something we don't know and have experienced something we have not experienced. The relationship opens us up to what they have got - it's all different.

Growth is all about something larger than you have got capacity for. It is not in the alignment of what you are already in, it is an expansion of what you are not in yet. The Holy Spirit is going to give you counsel; among other things, he will show you things to come. You do not have to be a prophet or psychic with a TV programme to operate in this because this is the privilege of the believer. Though a prophet has the responsibility and the gift capacity to be able to hear, see, perceive and take in information on an extraordinary level for the sake of others, you don't have to be a prophet to hear the thought of God - it is available for everyone.

We all have the latent capacity for deeper seeing, the effect of seeing deeply and hearing the thought of God is God-given.

Dynamic entrepreneurs will find what it means to have clarity, to act in the service of what is emerging; yet to emerge, they need new intuition and insight to create new realities. Scientists and entrepreneurs have to walk in these dimensions. One key to the deeper levels of learning is that the larger living whole, of which we are an active part, is not inherently static; like all living systems, they conserve features essential to their existence as they seek to evolve. Janos Salk, the inventor of the Polio vaccine spoke of tapping into the continuously unfolding dynamism of the universe and experiencing its evolution as an active process; a process that I can guide by the choices I make. He felt that this ability had enabled him to reject common wisdom and develop a vaccine that eventually saved millions of lives.

To lead from the future, you need to:

- Know who you are;
- Write the vision for your future;
- Write your growth program;
- Have strength and character in the area your assignment is requiring you to exercise it in;

Being perfect is not as important as being the person who shows up for the role you have got next. The questions you need to ask yourself are:

- Who do I have to be in the next session that I have never been before?
- Who do I have to become that I have never been?
- What will I be doing that I have never done?
- What will I need to know that I never learnt?
- What skill must I acquire that I never mastered?

In Daniel 1:8, innocent young Jews taken captive into Babylon made a choice not to become defiled by the King's meat. When you make a decision that you will walk pure, the intent of purity is priceless and God is able to keep you from failing; for some reason, God watches over the pure of heart and makes choices for them. Daniel was tested in verse 12, and proved to be healthy; at the end of 10 days, their features appeared better and fatter than all the youths eating the King's choice food. God gave Daniel and his cohorts knowledge, wisdom, skill and literature. They were tested in language and literature, arts, political matters, and in all areas of knowledge. God gave them supernatural abilities to compete and stay overboard among their equals.

You should align with the anointing for your assignment in the session you are in, so you can do the unusual. Enduring contradiction takes timing.

Sometimes it is not the vision that is wrong, it is the timing for its fulfilment. There were certain things I wanted to see happen when I was younger and it did not happen; now some of these things are starting to show up.

I am reminded of the story of Zechariah doing his priestly activity in Luke 1 - an angel visits him and foretells that he and his wife, Elizabeth, will have a son. Zechariah responds by asking questions and making statements that unauthorized the manifestation of the miracle. This is an interesting study of how works can affect manifestation. Zechariah questions were pregnant with the toxicity of unbelief. The angel replied and said you are going to be dumb and be unable to speak until the child is born. This was a protection against his talking his way out of the manifestation. Elizabeth delivers the baby. After the baby was delivered Zechariah was asked for the name of the baby and he writes his name is "John". Sometimes you cannot name the thing that heaven wants to do in your life until the period of contradiction is over. If you will endure the contradiction and keep your faith alive, you will be able to cooperate with divine timing. Don't be like Zechariah that had fallen out of faith with his own prayer.

FURTHER ACKNOWLEDGEMENTS

I wish to also thank the following people for promoting literacy, inspiring humanity to do better, and giving us the world that we have today:

- 1600 – Galileo Galilei discovers the principle of inertia, building the stage for a rational view of motion.
- 1600 – William Gilbert finds that Earth has magnetic poles and acts like a huge magnet.
- 1600 – Galileo Galilei discovers that projectiles move with a parabolic trajectory.
- 1608 – Hans Lippershey invents the refracting telescope, which Galileo Galilei soon puts to use.
- 1609 – Galileo Galilei observes moons of Jupiter, disproving church dogma that all movement in the universe is centred on Earth.
- 1609 – Johannes Kepler publishes his first two laws of planetary motion showing that planets move in elliptical orbits around the sun.
- 1610 – John Napier publishes tables of logarithms, showing how they can be used to accelerate calculations.
- 1619 – Kepler publishes his third law of planetary motion relating the time taken for a planet to orbit the sun with its distance from the sun.
- 1621 – Willebrord Snell discovers the laws of light refraction.
- 1628 – Kepler publishes his planetary tables, the calculations for which would have taken years without Napier's logarithms.
- 1629 – Nicolaus Cabeus finds there are two types of electric charge and notes both attractive and repulsive forces acting.
- 1632 – William Oughtred invents the slide rule. With the combined power of logarithms and slide rules, calculation speeds explode.
- 1632 – Galileo Galilei finds that the laws of motion are the same in all inertial reference frames.
- 1637 – René Descartes invents the Cartesian coordinate system – i.e. the x-y axis for graphs, allowing changes in quantities with time to be plotted.
- 1645 – Blaise Pascal invents the adding machine.

- 1652 – Thomas Bartholin discovers the human lymphatic system.
- 1662 – Robert Boyle publishes his law of pressure and volume in gases.
- 1654 – Blaise Pascal and Pierre de Fermat invent the mathematics of probability and statistics.
- 1656 – Christiaan Huygens discovers Saturn's rings after building a new telescope – the world's best.
- 1657 – Pierre de Fermat uses the principle of least time in optics.
- 1658 – Jan Swammerdam discovers the red blood cell.
- 1660 – Otto von Guerkicke builds a rotating sphere from which sparks fly. Static electricity can now be generated. He demonstrates electrostatic repulsion.
- 1660 – Robert Hooke discovers that the extension of a spring or elastic material is directly proportional to the applied force.
- 1661 – Robert Boyle writes The Skeptical Chymist, with his manifesto for the science of chemistry, explaining the roles of elements and compounds, and telling scientists they must carefully observe, record and report scientific data.
- 1633 – James Gregory publishes his design for the world's first reflecting telescope.
- 1664 – Robert Hooke uses a microscope to observe the cellular basis of life.
- 1665 – Isaac Newton invents calculus – the mathematics of change – without which we could not understand the modern world. He keeps it secret, using it to develop theories, which he eventually publishes in 1687.
- 1666 – Isaac Newton discovers that light is made up of all of the colours of the rainbow, which are refracted by different amounts in a glass prism.
- 1667 – Isaac Newton builds the world's first reflecting telescope.
- 1668 – John Wallis discovers the principle of conservation of momentum – one of the foundations of modern physics.
- 1669 – Hennig Brand becomes the first identifiable person to have discovered and isolated a new chemical element – phosphorus.
- 1674 – Antony van Leeuwenhoek discovers microorganisms.
- 1675 – Robert Boyle shows that electric repulsion and attraction act

in a vacuum.

- 1676 – Ole Christensen Roemer measures the speed of light for the first time.
- 1676 – Christiaan Huygens finds light can be refracted and diffracted, and should be considered to be a wave-like phenomenon.
- 1684 – Gottfried Leibniz publishes his calculus, which he discovered independently of Isaac Newton. He has been working on calculus for the past decade.
- 1687 – Isaac Newton publishes one of the most important scientific books ever: *Philosophiae Naturalis Principia Mathematica*, revolutionizing physics and our understanding of gravity and motion.

This was a momentous century in which science moved from a state of knowledge that was in many ways little more advanced than third century BC Greece, to a much more advanced, sophisticated position, paving the way for the industrial revolution in the 1700s, and many more famous scientists. Probably the greatest advantages that Renaissance scientists had over their ancient Greek predecessors were:

- The invention of the movable type printing press in 1450 by Johannes Gutenberg. (Bi Sheng invented movable type printing much earlier, in about 1040 AD in China, but this does not appear to have influenced the Renaissance).
- Leonardo Fibonacci brought the Hindu-Arabic number system to Europe in 1202 AD.

The Greek number system was primitive, making calculations cumbersome, and confining most Greek mathematical achievements to geometry. European scientists were using the Roman system, which was little better.

The familiar Hindu-Arabic system of 0,1,2,3,4,5,6,7,8,9 ... brought with it, ease of calculation, and the recognition that zero was a number in its own right. Mathematical rules for the correct use of zero, and negative numbers, were first written in 628 AD in Brahmagupta's book, Brahmasputha Siddhanta.

Following the huge scientific advances of the 1600s, we have continued to take enormous strides in scientific knowledge, carrying us to where we are today.

REFERENCES

PART ONE: THE FUNDAMENTALS

Payne, R. K. (2014) Framework for Understanding Poverty 5th Edition Audiobook

https://en.wikipedia.org/wiki/Cambridge_equation

http://thismatter.com/money/banking/money.htm

The Death of Money: The Coming Collapse of the International Monetary System Paperback – 5 Mar 2015 by James Rickards (Author); Publisher: Portfolio Penguin (5 Mar. 2015)

Leaf, C. (2009) Who Switched Off My Brain: Controlling Toxic Thoughts and Emotions. Thomas Nelson Publishers

Leaf, C. (2013) Switch On Your Brain: The Key to Peak Happiness, Thinking, and Health. Baker Book Publishers

http://drleaf.com/blog/think-and-eat-yourself-smart-prologue/

http://robmoore.com/blog/7-steps-to-finding-your-vision-true-purpose/

http://drleaf.com/blog/episode-3-mind-health-series/

http://searchnetworking.techtarget.com/news/450279989/Cisco-reorganization-to-make-engineering-more-nimble?utm_medium=EM&asrc=EM_NLN_55066398&utm_campaign=20160328_Cisco%20CEO%20Robbins%20splits%20engineering%20into%20four%20units_kfinnell&utm_source=NLN&track=NL-1817&ad=9067

Scott, S. (2014) Master Strategies of Super Achievers Program.

Sheets, D. (2001) God's Timing for Your Life: Seeing the Seasons of Your Life Through God's Eyes. Regal Books

Personal Power – Thoughts - Further research: 1 John 4:16,18, 5:18; Genesis 1:26; Luke 16:19-31; Hosea 4:6; Ecclesiastes 7:29; John 8:44; Romans 12:2; 2 Corinthians 10:5; Philippians 4:6-8; Isaiah 55:8-9; Romans 12:2; John 15:5; 2 Timothy 1:7; Mark 4:14-20; James 1:13-16; Matthew 5:48; 2 Corinthians 10:3-5; John 1:1; 1 Peter 5:6-10; Hebrews 12:1; Matthew 18:16, Romans 1:17; John 3:3; Acts 2:1-4; 1 Corinthians 12:4-11; Matthew 5:18; Proverbs 9:1-11; 2 Corinthians 3:18; Ephesians 4:16; Galatians 6:6-8; Mark 4:17-20; Deuteronomy 30:19, 1 Corinthians 2:16; Ephesians 3:10

Demartini, J. (2013) The Values Factor: The Secret to Creating an Inspired and Fulfilling Life. Penguin Books

Robbins, T. (2014) Money Master the Game: 7 Simple Steps to Financial Freedom. Simon & Schuster

The Power of Vulnerability: Teachings on Authenticity, Connection and Courage Audio CD – Audiobook, 7 Jan 2013 by Brene Brown (Author)

Canfield, J. (2014) The Success Principles: How to Get from Where You Are to Where You Want to Be, HarperCollins books

Carson, B. (1992) Think Big: Unleashing Your Potential for Excellence. Zondervan

Port, M. (2011) Book Yourself Solid: The Fastest, Easiest, and Most Reliable System for Getting More Clients Than You Can Handle Even if You Hate Marketing and Selling.

Business Secrets from the Bible: Spiritual Success Strategies for Financial Abundance 11 Apr 2014; by Rabbi Daniel Lapin

Warrillow, J. (2013) Built to Sell: Creating a Business That Can Thrive Without You Paperback, Penguin

Kaufman, J. (2012) The Personal MBA: A World-Class Business Education in a Single

Harnish, V. (2014) Scaling Up

Pierce, C.D. et al. (2011) A Time to Advance: Understanding the Significance of the Hebrew Tribes and Months. Glory of Zion International

Science Casts: Space-Time Vortex

https://www.youtube.com/watch?v=XkAPv5s92z0

https://www.generals.org/rpn/the-seven-mountains/

http://www.studymode.com/essays/Boeing-And-Airbus-Strategy-And-Vision-1123916.html

http://www.johnpratt.com/items/docs/lds/meridian/2003/exodus.html

Biltz, M. (2014) Blood Moons: Decoding the Imminent Heavenly Signs. WND Books.

https://lancewallnau.com/

https://en.wikipedia.org/wiki/Seed_money

www.moneychimp.com

https://www.fool.com/

PART TWO: THE MODEL

http://www.qdistrategies.com/resources/

Aaker, David A. (1996). Building Strong Brands. The Free Press: New York

Gassmann, O et al. (2014) The Business Model Navigator: 55 Models That Will Revolutionise Your Business Paperback; Publisher: FT Publishing International

Moore, R. (2015) Life Leverage: How to get more done in less time, outsource everything and create your ideal mobile lifestyle

http://www.qdistrategies.com/tools/value-management/

http://blog.strategyzer.com/posts/2015/12/17/10-essential-links-for-testing-your-value-proposition-business-models

http://www.panozzaj.com/blog/2012/01/11/signs-you-arent-really-building-a-minimum-viable-product/?_sm_au_=i2VTNrH6VkMrDHRr

http://blog.strategyzer.com/posts/2016/4/18/how-to-convince-leaders-to-avoid-business-plans-when-validating-new-ideas

https://www.marsdd.com/mars-library/crafting-your-value-proposition/

https://www.marsdd.com/mars-library/value-proposition-a-reflection-of-the-relationship-between-your-customer-and-brand/

http://suitcaseentrepreneur.com/live/tse-116-denise-duffield-thomas/#disqus_thread

https://gigaom.com/2010/12/20/flo-tv-fail/

https://hbr.org/2014/12/build-an-innovation-engine-in-90-days

https://vimeo.com/163412281

Dr. David Garvin and Dr. Amy Edmonson, Article: "Is Yours a Learning Organization?"

Osterwalder, A. et al. (2014) Value Proposition Design: How to Create Products and Services Customers Want (Strategyzer). John Wiley & Sons;

Osterwalder, A. et al. (2010) Business Model Generation: A Handbook for Visionaries, Game Changers, and Challengers

Llewellyn-Davies, D. (2013) BGI Strategy on a Page: Develop Your Business Strategy on just One Single Page. BGI, Filament Publishing

https://hbr.org/2017/07/how-to-set-more-realistic-growth-targets

www.discoverydrivengrowth.com

https://www.ritamcgrath.com/books/the-entrepreneurial-mindset/

ABOUT THE AUTHOR

Chukwudi C. Samuel is an entrepreneur, award-winning author and international speaker. Starting with nothing, he built successful businesses in the UK and Africa. Through personal experience and working with and interviewing some of the world's most successful people, Chukwudi discovered that there is a proven blueprint that top entrepreneurs, business owners and leader use to scale up their life and businesses without comprising key personal relationships

Chukwudi Samuel is one of today's most innovative wealth experts and accelerates the conversation about wealth. He continues to expand his horizons through his tenacity and absolute confidence in what he teaches and demonstrates. His most significant accomplishment is probably similar to yours: being a devoted parent, son and a friend. He enjoys photography and supports several charities. Chukwudi holds a computer engineering degree and a University of Bradford MBA. He has worked and consulted as a Strategy Managing Consultant, Solution Architect, Business and Enterprise Architect. He maintains CCIE #16352, ITIL, TOGAF and other certifications.

99344363R00120

Made in the USA
Columbia, SC
08 July 2018